Folk Magic

The Ultimate Guide to Norse Paganism, Brujeria, Curanderismo, Scottish Witchcraft, Jewish Magic, Kabbalah, Druidry, and African American Spirituality

Your Free Gift
(only available for a limited time)

Thanks for getting this book! If you want to learn more about various spirituality topics, then join Mari Silva's community and get a free guided meditation MP3 for awakening your third eye. This guided meditation mp3 is designed to open and strengthen ones third eye so you can experience a higher state of consciousness. Simply visit the link below the image to get started.

https://spiritualityspot.com/meditation

Table of Contents

Introduction

When you think of magical practices, European and Middle Eastern traditions often come to mind. These usually encompass Wiccan magic practices, Paganism, Druidism, and other neopagan systems. However, throughout history, magical practices have been a part of numerous other cultures. So, to imagine that all magic practices boil down to pagan concepts is a tempting yet misdirected notion. For that reason, it's critical to include vibrant folk magic traditions such as Voodoo, Hoodoo, Curanderismo, Brujeria, and Kabbalah magic, alongside Celtic and Norse magic. Most folk magic books out there only focus on well-known cultures that practice magic, omitting the less common ones. By contrast, this book will highlight each culture and the associated magical practices in extensive detail.

Paganism, witchcraft, and other magical practices have been around for much longer than one might think. Surprisingly, these practices are now more popular than ever before. False notions of witchcraft and magical practices have been common throughout history. In the past, those suspected of engaging in it faced dangerous consequences, excommunication, and even death. Today, fortunately, many magical practices are carried out openly without fear. Whether it's Jewish mystic and occult teachings or Celtic practices, many people are eagerly learning the practices and teachings of these ancient belief systems.

Whether you want to learn about the magic practices of Celtic culture or wish to familiarize yourself with Scottish witchcraft, this book will be the perfect guide for you. For someone interested in magic practices but unsure where to start this journey, reading this book will provide you with just enough knowledge about the various folk magic traditions to make an informed decision. Even if you're interested in a single culture, a lot of information is provided for each one, along with its fundamental concepts and traditions.

The opening chapter will guide you in choosing which folk magic culture you identify with most, while the following chapters will cover each specific folk magic culture. Every chapter details the history and development of that culture and the belief system they follow. The traditions and holidays observed by these cultures will also be discussed in detail to give you a complete idea of what it's like in practice. While you might feel that a single chapter cannot cover a particular culture comprehensively, it provides all the necessary fundamentals to discover and connect with it.

This book does not claim to make you a master of folk magic within a few weeks. Instead, it promises that once you've read it, you'll have enough knowledge about each kind of folk magic to decide based on your preference. The best part? We've included a section dedicated at the end of each chapter with self-reflective questions to help you decide which culture you feel attracted to intuitively. Without further ado, if you're ready to delve into the world of folk magic and uncover its deepest secrets, let's get started!

Chapter 1: Folk Magic Basics

As you study magic and navigate through this fascinating topic, the term "folk magic" will surely come up. As it happens, there's always a great deal of curiosity around folk magic and its practitioners. People often confuse it with witchcraft, and some even believe practitioners are necessarily religious and worship a specific lord. Others believe that people who practice this magic are polytheistic or nature worshippers.

Some believe that people who practice this magic are polytheistic or nature worshippers.
https://www.pexels.com/photo/woman-in-traditional-wear-11960754/

There's a reason why folk magic is often associated with religion and gods. Modern practitioners working with magico-religion have adopted folk magic in their practices, resulting in many misconceptions about this practice. However, folk magic is different from magical practices associated with religion, such as Druidry, Wicca, and Shamanism. In this first chapter, we will clear any misconceptions you may have about folk magic and explain what makes it different from other types of magic.

Folk Magic Explained

Despite being one of the oldest magical practices in the world, folk magic has managed to adapt to modern practices and other cultures. Essentially, folk magic is an umbrella term that encompasses various magical practices. What distinguishes these practices from other types of magic is that they're all practiced by the common folk. In other words, it isn't a type of ceremonial magic that requires specific skills or a professional practitioner.

Folk magic differs from other types of magic mainly due to its practicability. It focuses on practical issues and helping people and the community. For example, it can help women struggling with fertility, bring good luck, help people find love, drive evil spirits away, cure diseases, and help retrieve lost objects. Since this type of magic was practiced by common folks who were often illiterate back then, it relied on oral traditions, and the spells were simple enough for them to memorize. Working with folk magic isn't complicated since most of the materials needed are common and include wood, nails, plants, eggshells, stones, coins, and twine.

The History of Folk Magic

By definition, folk practices are old, maybe even ancient. For instance, Scottish folk magic can be traced back to the old way of life. Different cultures influenced this particular tradition, including the Saxons, Angles, Gaelic, Pictish, Norman, and Norse. It borrowed from ancient mythologies and traditions until it formed its own combination of folklore and myth. Although folk magic has developed, become independent, and created its own folklore and mythology, it still holds on to its original system of culture and politics.

Luckily, folk magic hasn't disappeared in the confines of history, as many literal folks were able to preserve it by writing it down. Today, we know about their rituals, prayers, practices, beliefs, festivals, celebrations, and songs. For example, one of the more interesting practices passed down to us is "Ranns." The folks sang these special songs before bedtime, when waking up, when sowing seeds, and before picking plants.

The Main Characteristics of Folk Magic

Folk magic has many distinguishable traits. For starters, it's a simple practice available to the greatest number, it's often practiced orally, and it helps with issues that people deal with in their daily lives. Practitioners also customize the rituals and items they use based on the target of their spell. This is meant to link the target and symbols together.

Generally speaking, spells in folk magic use various elements from nature, like water, stones, and plants. For instance, practitioners use stones to help the ill, tie pieces of cloth onto sacred wells for faster healing, and use Holy stones as tools to see into the world of the spirits. Another trait that distinguishes folk magic is that it can be practiced with any type of readily available tool. Unlike many other practices, rituals also don't play a great role in folk magic.

That is the beauty of folk magic – it's straightforward, and since it's the magic of the common folk, it doesn't require anything special or over the top. Every practitioner can choose the methods they see fit. This type of practical magic is ideal for normal daily needs and can be practiced with minimal effort.

Folk Magic vs. Witchcraft and Ceremonial Magic

As established, folk magic differs from Druidry, Wicca, and Witchcraft. Each of these types of magic has its own beliefs and traditions. However, all were heavily influenced by folk magic. More often than not, people treat witchcraft as an umbrella term that comprises all types of magic. However, witchcraft is its own type and differs from other types of magic, especially folk magic.

It's hard to compare folk magic with witchcraft since folk practitioners are not interested in witches. In fact, they consider them evil. This is something significant in folk magic beliefs that's useful to remember if you ever encounter folk practitioners. Some practitioners, especially Scottish ones, consider it offensive to compare or affiliate them with witches. Unlike witchcraft, folk magic isn't associated with or influenced by religion. They don't worship a specific deity and don't have to follow a specific set of beliefs to practice this type of magic. Since folk magic is ancient, its approaches and ideas haven't borrowed anything from modern religions. However, several folk magic practices preserved in literary works were later Christianized.

It's common knowledge how magic and those who practiced it or were suspected of practicing it were treated in Europe back in the day. Some even claimed that Christians believed folk magic was the same as witchcraft and prosecuted its practitioners. However, there's no factual truth to these claims. Witchcraft and folk magic are often opposites. Folk practitioners were respected in their communities, as the main purpose of their magic was to help and heal people. On the other hand, Witchcraft didn't serve the community and was often regarded as evil or harmful.

Witchcraft, Wicca, and other types of magic have borrowed various techniques from ceremonial magic, such as invoking gods and goddesses or forming circles to practice magic. By contrast, folk magic doesn't use any of these techniques or borrow from ceremonial magic. Ceremonial magic is also known for its use of rituals, another aspect that distinguishes it from folk magic. Unlike folk magic, practitioners of ceremonial magic need certain tools and accessories for practice, referred to as ceremonial weapons.

Cunning Folk

If you type "folk magic" on any search engine, you'll find the words "cunning folk" frequently coming up. Who were the cunning folk, and how were they associated with folk magic? The term cunning folk describes diviners, folk magic practitioners, and healers who lived in Europe during the Middle Ages, all through the 20th century. For centuries, the cunning folk worked to help their communities by providing various services that often involved magic. These folks were hard workers who did everything they could to help their communities and even neighboring ones. They would travel for miles to help the sick, provide a sympathetic ear and a shoulder to cry on to those in need, and use their magic to help the afflicted. Any modern-day magic practitioner is influenced by cunning folk. These wise men and women were highly respected and known for their immense knowledge.

As it happens, cunning folks didn't name themselves as such. It was historians who referred to them by that unflattering denomination. Cunning folks played a significant role in the magic world, and everyone knew at least one cunning folk. They were treated differently from others who practiced magic, as they weren't witches or associated with witchcraft. People saw their magic as helpful rather than evil.

Practicing folk magic allowed these gifted individuals to help others and find solutions to the problems common people encountered. This is why the term is often associated with folk magic because many of its practitioners were cunning folks and used their magic benevolently. However, unlike other folk magic practitioners, the cunning folk were literate. The folk magic practiced by this group traveled beyond Europe and became popular in other parts of the world, notably North America.

Folk Magic Cultural Path

Now that you're familiar with the concept of folk magic, you probably wonder how you can start practicing. Although folk magic doesn't seem complicated, since it's the magic of the people, it does have one major challenge beginners often encounter. Folk magic practitioners struggle to find the right cultural path for them. In this dedicated section, we will focus on folk magic cultural paths so you can choose the one that suits you best.

Hoodoo

Hoodoo is one of the traditional folk magic and rootwork practices. The word "Hoodoo" doesn't mean the same thing to everyone but depends on the type of practice and practitioners. It's often referred to as rootwork or conjures. Hoodoo originated in various African practices during the 19th century. It found its way to the United States, merging with popular magical practices, including European folklore and Native American. While this syncretism of practices may seem rather uncommon, it was the foundation from which contemporary Hoodoo evolved.

Since Hoodoo's birthplace in Africa, many of its practitioners are African-Americans. However, people from different cultures and backgrounds follow this practice as well. Some Hoodoo practitioners have learned this practice from their relatives, as it's often passed down from one generation to the next. The practice of traditional Hoodoo has remained the same ever since it originated.

Since Hoodoo is a branch of folk magic, most of its spells are practical ones that involve lust, love, and money. Although Hoodoo isn't a pagan practice and its followers don't worship any deities, some highly revere their ancestors. That said, a large number of its practitioners are devout Christians. In some regions in the United States, people practice mountain magic, which they usually refer to as Hoodoo. Practitioners of this type of Hoodoo incorporate various tools into their practice, like charms, amulets, and omens.

It's essential to note that Hoodoo and Voodoo are two distinct practices. They're easy to confuse due to similar spellings, but the two couldn't be more different. Voodoo revolves around religious practices and worshiping various deities that aren't associated with folk magic. However, they share the same background, as both originated in Africa.

If you plan on practicing Hoodoo magic, you should begin by reading about the history of Africans and the struggles and trauma they faced due to their enslavement.

Pow-wow

Often referred to as "braucherei," Pow-wow is another type of folk magic. This practice focuses on healing the sick and making remedies. Americans of German descent who lived in Pennsylvania were the first to practice this type of magic. The charms, remedies, and rituals found in Pow-wow originated in Europe and later found their way to the United States, specifically Pennsylvania. This interesting name comes from the Algonquian language and refers to a healing ritual.

Incidentally, a popular practice among Native Americans goes by the same name, which often causes confusion among magical practitioners. However, Pow-wow folk magic is different from its namesake. The European settlers who mingled with Native Americans adopted the term Pow-wow, which described a healing ritual. The Native American Pow-wow involves a gathering of people from various cultures where they dance, sing, celebrate, and practice rituals. However, both practices share their etymology. Nowadays, practitioners prefer the term braucherei to differentiate between folk magic Pow-wow and the Native American version.

Back in the 17th century, many Native Americans lived in Pennsylvania. Various tribes resided on-site, while other tribes visited the region occasionally. In the late 17th century and throughout the 18th century, European settlers made their way to Pennsylvania. Some of these settlers were German, and these newcomers had their own religion, beliefs, and traditions. As a result, their magical practices were mainly religious. Religion played a significant role in their practices as they highly revered the Catholic Saints, and prayers and blessings were a great part of their lives. Healing practices often involved herbal remedies, invoking a god, and Holy objects. They used and continue to use sacred symbols to protect themselves, their families, and their homes. Farmers still decorate their barns using various hex signs to invoke protection.

The religious influence over Pow-wow didn't die down over the years. In fact, practitioners have relied on the Bible and incorporated various verses in their practices. Magic and religion were very much integrated, as practitioners believed that only God could provide healing. According to their beliefs, there was no better or more effective way to practice healing folk magic than scripture. Pow-wow practitioners often used charms and spells that belonged to the Catholics who lived in medieval Europe. Back then, these Catholics used these spells and charms as protection against evil magic and witchcraft. For example, they used them to protect their cattle, stop bleeding, treat burns, protect against thefts, cure fevers, and as a good luck charm before a court.

Pow-wow is still a common practice favored by many practitioners to this day. Male practitioners are called Braucher, while female practitioners are called Braucherin. In other communities around Pennsylvania, they're referred to as Pow-wowers or Pow-wow doctors, owing to their status as healers. Pow-wow, like folk magic, relied mainly on oral tradition. Spells, rituals, charms, and prayers were never written down but passed down orally from one generation to the next. Male practitioners taught female practitioners, and vice-versa. Practitioners of this type of magic believed that only students who wanted to help others and make a difference in the world should learn Pow-wow. They memorize their prayers and rituals and vow to share them with those they believe were chosen by God to provide healing to the sick.

There are certain rules every Pow-wow practitioner should abide by:

- Under no circumstances should practitioners get paid for their services

- You should never reveal the name of the person who introduced you to Pow-wow

- To practice Pow-wow, you should be a Christian who worships the Christian God and follow the teachings of the Bible

Now that you're familiar with folk magic's main types and cultural paths, you can choose the one you feel most connected to. If you can't decide, you can apply eclectic magic and mix both traditions. That said, before deciding on a cultural path, it's wise to investigate your family tree to learn more about your cultural heritage. This step is necessary to help you choose the appropriate culture and put you on the right path. Belief is another strong tool that can guide you toward the right choice. In fact, belief and intention are essential elements in all types of magic, including folk magic. Intention, belief, and exploring your family tree are the main factors that can help anyone decide which culture to follow.

Choosing a cultural path is only the beginning of your journey. The next step is learning as much as possible about that culture. So, conduct further research by reading about your chosen culture's history, beliefs, customs, and traditions. While you can find many helpful resources online, it's best to enlist the help of practitioners in your community. You can talk to them, seek their advice, ask them questions, and give yourself a chance to learn firsthand from experienced practitioners. If any relatives are practitioners, they can also provide useful information about your family tree and various cultural paths.

This chapter is only the beginning of a personal, fascinating journey. The upcoming chapters will each cover the most widespread folk practices. The beneficial knowledge you'll come across will come in handy as you embark on your journey as a magic folk practitioner.

Magic can be a force for good or evil, depending on your chosen practice and how you plan on using it. Folk magic has proven to be a force for good over the centuries. People eager to help others and serve their community practice this magic and try to set themselves apart from witchcraft or any type of magic that doesn't benefit humanity or the greater good. Folk magic is the magic of the common folk, where healers devote their lives to easing people's pain, providing comfort, and ensuring their safety.

Chapter 2: African Spirituality

African spirituality is a broad umbrella that includes numerous traditions with several customs and spiritual beliefs. This chapter will delve into the basics of African spirituality. In this chapter, you'll learn about the origins of African spirituality and how various external forces influenced our modern perception of this system. You'll come across a few of Africa's most popular principal traditions and belief systems and understand their characteristics and main beliefs. Finally, you'll learn about the African pantheon, its most popular deities, and the most common methods of worship.

African spirituality is a broad umbrella that includes numerous traditions with several customs and spiritual beliefs.
https://www.pexels.com/photo/person-holding-lighted-candle-in-dark-room-6144036/

The Origins of African Spirituality

African spirituality is the melting pot of numerous cultures, nations, and traditions. It combines all that is natural and supernatural. Even as Islam and Christianity arrived on the continent, practitioners of African spirituality managed to get around these doctrines by incorporating them into their spiritual system with their deities and beliefs. Despite the continent's exceptional diversity, it still maintains some intrinsic similarities.

Since Africa was subject to colonialism throughout the centuries, African deities, folklore, legends, traditions, and beliefs were sullied, often forcefully, by outsiders. However, in most cases, natives were able to keep some parts of their practices intact. Many of the ancient core African beliefs are still prominent to this day.

Most African spiritual systems believe in the existence of one supreme god. For them, this divine force reigns over all living beings and non-living objects in all of the universe and the heavens. This god is also thought to be the ruler of the deities and spirits in the spiritual realm. They also believe in ancestor veneration, which is why the elderly are treated with the utmost respect. African spirituality suggests that there's an afterlife, which explains why practitioners conduct animal sacrifice after someone passes. They believe it allows the deceased to easily journey into the ancestral realm.

Many African cultures also conduct rites of passage and celebratory rituals for birth, entering adulthood, and death. When individuals enter puberty, they are celebrated with an initiation phase that includes rituals, passing tribal secrets and knowledge on to them, and male circumcision. Folklore typically approaches witchcraft with amazement, regarding it with a level of caution and fear as well. Non-practitioners usually use the term "witch doctor" to refer to spiritual practitioners, prophets, shamans, and traditional healers. However, in African culture, there is a great distinction between these entities and practices like black magic, sorcery, and witchcraft.

Several African spiritual systems are influenced and even based on Africanized versions of foreign world religions. African religious origins majorly rely on oral transmissions. It would be challenging to successfully portray oral-literary traditions in written form because they are not novel-like but rather take after animated plays. The messages would be grasped more effectively via performances instead of written stories. These pieces would lose their meaning, overtones, subtleties, vividness, and clarity if not accompanied by traditional dances, sound, voice, facial expressions, and body language.

There aren't any written ancient texts to guide modern practitioners through spiritual practices. They only conducted rituals and practiced oral transmissions, often done secretly after Christianity and Islam swept across the continent. Unfortunately, many foreign historical writers aimed to glorify their achievements and display their self-proclaimed moral superiority by depicting ancient African spirituality practices as savage, barbarian, sinful, and uncivilized.

For years, this was the world's perception of African spirituality, as there were no countering opinions from the practitioners themselves. Ancient African nations were subject to genocides and cruelty from outsiders who went on religious and colonial conquests.

Ancient African spiritualists didn't have to record their beliefs in writing because each group had its own expert storytellers who passed the practice down through generations. Trained storytellers acted as the scribes and priests of the time. They educated people about the heritage and history of their belief system to perpetuate it.

Although this system worked for centuries, it became a problem when the tribes started breaking away from each other. Only a few old traces of history remained with them. For instance, the ancient South African Nguni peoples only know that their ancestors were from the "north" and resided near the great lakes. The more they split up and traveled further away, the shorter and vaguer their stories became. Their history was starting to be replaced by newer events.

It's believed that the myths, tales, and deities of Africans spiritually arose during that time. During this period, people were forced to think more pragmatically and reflect on their experiences. They began using animal metaphors and symbols to teach moral lessons, myths, origin stories, deities, and belief systems. They also used storytelling to explain the origins of the world and creation and why everything is exactly the way it is.

The elderly instructed their extended family all about etiquette and moral lessons. Another reason the elderly were esteemed members of society is that they took up the role of community and family philosophers, advisors, and mentors. Even kings and tribe chiefs created councils that comprised elderly members for personal guidance and advice.

According to African culture, spirituality relates to every aspect of life. It can't be set apart from the mundane. Some researchers today reject this idea and suggest that diaspora Africans influenced ancient traditions with modern religious perceptions. However, in reality, we don't know how accurate our knowledge of ancient African myths and deities is. Storytellers perform generational stories the way they were taught. No one can guarantee that intentional changes were made and details were lost over the years. Besides, the evolution of dialects makes it difficult to trace the exact origins of these tales, along with African deities.

Main Traditions in African Spirituality

The following are some of the main traditions in African spirituality:

Kemetism

Kemetism is the revived form of the ancient Egyptian belief system known as Egyptian Neopaganism or Neterism. There are numerous groups of practitioners of Kemetic spirituality, each of which takes on a different spiritual approach.

The term "Kemetism" is derived from the word Kemet, the ancient Egyptian name for Egypt. Practitioners of this religion aim to practice ancient Egyptian spiritual rituals and beliefs. Ancient Egyptian spirituality is an extremely complex topic that many historians still haven't gotten to grips with. That said, the practitioners of Kemetism completely trust what they understand.

The core belief of Kemetism is the concept of Ma'at, which is the idea of divine balance. It's believed to be the guiding and driving force of the universe. Ma'at, the goddess, provides 42 laws that touch upon ethical and moral guidelines that a person should follow to be rebirthed in the afterlife. They also believe in Netjer, who is considered the only supreme being. According to ancient Egyptian mythology, all deities in the pantheon are manifestations of this supreme god.

Some Kemetic beliefs are highly controversial. For instance, while some practitioners believe that it's a polytheistic religion, which allows them to worship several gods, others suggest that it's a monotheistic belief system. This debate is the result of Netjer's nature. While he is a single supreme god, he still has several manifestations. Many Kemetic individuals also believe in ancestral veneration and often pray to their ancestors for guidance. Anyone can become Kemetic, as it doesn't require a specific initiation procedure.

Vodou

Also known as Voodoo or Vodoun, Vodou is a religion that combines native African spiritual beliefs and Roman Catholicism. The native African portion of the belief system comes from the religion of the West African Dahomey people. This belief system is currently practiced in New Orleans, Haiti, and other regions in the Caribbean.

Vodou started when African slaves brought their traditional beliefs with them to the "New World." However, since their owners prohibited them from maintaining their spiritual practices, they resorted to finding their gods in Catholic saints. They also used the imagery found in the Catholic Church to practice their native rituals. Vodou practitioners can choose to be Christians but generally adhere to the Catholic denomination; in that case, they may consider spirits and saints to be the same thing.

Vodou practitioners are monotheistic and believe in a single supreme god, known as Bondye. They also believe in the existence of lesser prominence beings, known as the Iwa. These are divided into the families of Ghede, Rada, and Petro, who are more involved in daily life. The Iwa and humans have a reciprocal connection, where the Iwa offer practitioners their assistance in exchange for food and offerings. They also believe in the existence of the afterlife. They think that a person's souls linger around until they experience rebirth after their death. If you wish to practice Voodoo, you need to engage in an extensive initiation period.

Santeria

Like Vodou, Santeria is a syncretic religion. It blends Yoruban spirituality, which comes from West Africa, traditional Caribbean influences, and aspects of Catholicism. It was also created when enslaved Africans were sent to work in the Caribbean.

Enslaved people also deemed it safer to worship saints as symbols of their ancestral Yoruban orishas or divine entities. According to Yoruban traditions, the orishas are messengers between the divine realm and the world of humans. This belief system relies on magical practices to invoke the orishas via divination methods, ritualistic practices, sacrifices, possession, and trances.

Many Americans practice Santeria today with the guidance of a high priest, especially when ceremonies or rituals are conducted. Before they are initiated, a Santero or high priest must undergo a testing period and meet certain requirements, including counseling and practicing divination and herbalism. The orishas are the ones who determine whether the candidate is a good fit for the priesthood.

The Orishas include Elegua (a messenger between humans and the divine), Yemaya (the essence of motherhood), Babalu Aye (the "Father of the World"), Chango (the embodiment of sexuality and masculine energy), and Oya, the guardian of those who have passed on. Each of these Orishas is the Santerian equivalent of a prominent Catholic figure or saint.

Santeria doesn't concern itself much with the afterlife. Rather, it focuses on the present moment and natural forces. Each of the Santerian deities represents a certain aspect or element of nature, like air, or a human trait, like power. To practice Santeria, you must complete a series of initiation rites.

The African Pantheon

The term "African Pantheon" comprises numerous tribes, belief systems, and deities. Most African spiritual belief systems have their own pantheons. For instance, the Vodou pantheon consists of 8 deities - Legba, Ayizan, Damballah, Egwe, Zaka, Egou, Guede, and Rzulie (Freda) Dahomey. Some religions believe in one supreme deity, like Juok, Roog, Olodumare, Nyame, and Chukwu, and they all generally possess similar traits. Since we cannot include all African gods in this chapter, we've gathered ten of the most powerful African deities. This section is a good starting point for the African pantheons and can give insight into the characteristics of significant African deities.

Sango

Sango is the Orisha of thunder. He is known for his ability to strike anyone who commits a crime with thunder and lightning. If the criminal is a thief, then the item they stole would be placed down on their chest, then they are struck down. Besides being considered the most powerful African god, he is among the most popular across the globe. Sango is the deity of numerous affairs, including maintaining social order, vengeance, and protection. He is believed to announce his presence by instigating a thunderstorm.

Nana Buluku

Nana Buluku is an African goddess and the Fon's people supreme Goddess. Although the Fon comes from the Ewes of Togo and Benin, Nana Buluku's prominence extends far beyond the border of these regions. While the Yorubas call her by that name, the Igbos refer to her as Olisabuluwa. She is believed to be the mother of the twin god of the Sun and the Moon, Mawu-Lisa.

Mawu-Lisa

Mawu-Lisa is a twin deity believed to be both female and male. Their Mawu aspect is the deity of the Moon, and Lisa is the deity of the Sun. They are responsible for maintaining order in the world.

Alekwu

Alekwu is one of the gods the Northern Nigerian Idoma peoples worship. He is a powerful deity known for settling disputes, protecting, and keeping social order. It's believed that this deity can hunt down and murder his enemy in one to three weeks. He is a feared punisher to those who commit or serve as accomplices to any crime. His followers believe that he is omnipresent, meaning that distance won't stop him from protecting or punishing people.

Inkosazana

Also known as Nomkhubuluwana, Inkosazana is the Zulu deity of agriculture and fertility. Her followers refer to her as the "Mermaid," as they believe she resides in water and manifests herself in that form and in the form of other animals. She is the protector of all and makes her presence known only to those who are pure at heart. She appears in dreams, misty clouds, and foggy waters and heals those who are ill.

Sho'risdal

This Berber goddess is a very compassionate being. She is believed to be the mother of abundance and life. The change of seasons is said to be instigated by her mood swings. Ironically, this deity of life and bounty is the wife of Vyinsul, the deity of death.

Ngai

The Kikuyus consider Ngai to be the god of all creation. He lives on African mountains and manifests himself through natural and celestial entities like the stars, moon, wind, rain, and sun. The Kikuyus also believe he lives in fig trees, which is why they make sacrifices for him there. Ngai is also believed to be responsible for human deaths.

Heka

Heka is among the earliest ancient Egyptian gods. He performed magic and healed people. He also pioneered the caduceus symbol, the popular image of two snakes swirling around a pole, which portrayed his power. This symbol is now associated with the Greek god Hermes.

Mamlambo

Mamlambo is the South African and Zulu goddess of the rivers. She is thought to manifest as a giant snake that lives in the water. She has the power to grant wealth but is also able to cast horrid misfortunes. It's believed that Mamlambo feeds on the brains and faces of her victims.

Achamán

The Guanches people of Tenerife Island followed Achamán, the supreme god. He is considered the creator of air, land, and fire. He is responsible for breathing life into all creatures. Although he lives somewhere way above, he often descends to Earth to get in touch with his creations.

Eshu

Eshu is the African god of trickery and mischief, similar to the popular Norse god Loki. Unlike other trickster gods in various mythologies worldwide, Eshu is neither evil nor malicious. He doesn't spend his days playing tricks, nor does he enjoy mankind's suffering. Eshu acts as a messenger traveling between the physical and other worlds. This divine trickster has a devilish side, though. If a person or another deity doesn't acknowledge his presence, he is known to react unkindly toward them. He prefers offerings like tobacco.

Ogun

Ogun is the African god of war and iron. He is known as a warrior and always carries some of the finest weapons in heaven and earth. He exercises his role as the god of war and iron by blessing the weapons. According to African mythology, Ogun was the one who taught mankind how to make weapons using iron. He doesn't have a say in what a person chooses to do with these weapons. Ogun is a deity who doesn't interfere in the affairs of mankind. Many people pray to him and celebrate him in a festival every year.

Oshun

Oshun is the African goddess of the river. She is one of Shango's wives and the one closest to his heart. This river goddess is highly revered among the African people as they believe she has bestowed them with the Niger River, one of their most significant rivers. She blesses her people by keeping the rivers clean and ensuring they never run out of fish. This shows how much she cares about mankind. Oshun is also associated with childbirth and fertility. She is always depicted, showing her motherly and caring side.

Oya

Oya is the goddess of the weather and also one of Shango's wives. She is associated with the wind and has power over the clouds as well. She is one of the most powerful deities, as she can create cyclones and hurricanes. The African people believe that she causes destruction with Shango during thunderstorms. Oya also plays a role in the spirit realm as she provides help to the spirits of the dead as they begin their journey into the otherworld.

Yemaya

Yemaya is the African goddess of the ocean and the mother of all living things. Similar to Oshun, Yemayais is a caring mother, and she is fiercely protective of her children. In fact, she is the mother of all living beings. When someone is sad, she is always there for them, providing comfort and taking away their pain. Women who suffer from fertility issues often pray to her. She is a patient and loving goddess who rarely gets angry. However, when she does, she becomes a force for destruction. Thanks to her immense power and status, Yemaya is highly revered.

Modjaji

Modjaji is the goddess of rain, meaning she has the power to make the skies rain or prevent it and cause drought. She is one of the oldest goddesses, but the African people believe that her spirit lives in a young woman, and she now walks among them.

Oba

Another of Shango's wives, Oba, is the orisha of manifestation and water. Although she is a goddess, she still experiences human emotions. She was jealous of how much Shango loved Oshun. She went to her and asked why Shango loved her more than his other wives. Oshun was cunning and told Oba that she cut her ear and then made it into a powder-like substance to add to Shango's food. Oba believed Oshun's false story and did the same thing. However, when Shango found out, he sent her to earth. She turned into a river that was named after her.

Obaluaye

Obaluaye is the orisha of miracles and healing in African mythology. He is highly revered among his people, yet they are also terrified of him. Obaluaye can heal any ailments, but he can just as easily curse those who anger him. He can cure any disease, but he usually focuses on dying patients.

Obatala

Obatala is the father of the sky, the creator of mankind, and Yemaya's husband. He is a merciful god who represents purity and peace. Obatala is fair, which is why the orishas often seek his help and wisdom during conflicts. In African mythology, the people believed that all mankind's heads belonged to him since he was the creator.

Traditional Methods of Worship

Each belief system comes with a unique set of rites, rituals, practices, and methods of worship. However, most share the following characteristics:

Sacrifices

African spiritual systems often include the practice of sacrifices, which requires slaughtering an animal, bird, and sometimes even a human to honor a deity. Practitioners mindfully select their sacrifice to offer their bloodshed to appease a deity. The animals sacrificed must be of one solid color and are given back to a deity as a sign of appreciation for everything that they have done for them.

Sacrifices are considered an act of thankfulness or gratefulness. People also conduct sacrifices to earn god's forgiveness after committing wrongdoing. Sacrifices are thought to make a deity help their followers during challenging periods in life and serve as an invitation for the deity to partake in family and social gatherings. They can help practitioners maintain a good relationship with their deities and ask them to prevent perils such as floods, droughts, and epidemics.

Sacrifices are also conducted during rites of passage like birth, initiation, adulthood, marriage, and death. It was also believed that sacrifices could help alleviate the intensity of disasters and were commonly made after abundant harvests and before wars. Sacrifices weren't uncommon in the selection process of leaders, as well as cleansing and reconciliation ceremonies.

Heads of families, practitioners of medicines, and priests were the only elected members of society to conduct sacrifices. They have to accompany the process with prayers.

Offerings

Offerings are another means of worship. These require practitioners to provide their deity with milk, honey, or other food and beverage items. Offerings should be mindfully selected to suit the liking and preferences of the deity being worshiped.

Singing and Dancing

Practitioners frequently perform native songs and dances during communal worship. This practice serves to honor and thank a deity and strengthen the performer's emotional connection with them. Practitioners supplement their performances with drums, musical instruments, and hand clapping. Singing and dancing help instill a sense of community and solidarity among practitioners.

Prayers

Prayers are verbal interactions with a deity and are often short and straightforward. Most religious groups pray during significant occasions. One can pray while standing, prostrating, raising a hand, kneeling, bowing, or facing a specifically identified direction.

Invocations

Invocations are brief, formal, and concise forms of prayers. One may use this act of worship to address god, ask them for guidance, request their help, and more.

Blessings

Blessings are often conducted by elders and incorporate aspects of prayer. According to some belief systems, a person doing the blessing is doing so on behalf of a deity.

Salutations

As the name suggests, this method of worship involves addressing and saluting a god. For instance, a salutation would be "Dear God," etc.

Questions for Self-Reflection

- Do I have any African ancestors?

- Which African deities resonate with me the most?

- How do I feel about the mixing of different religious and cultural traditions?

Now that you've read this chapter, you have enough knowledge about African spirituality to determine whether this is the right belief system for you. The material covered here is a comprehensive starting point for your African spirituality journey and lays a good foundation for further research.

Chapter 3: Brujeria and Curanderismo

Brujeria and Curanderismo are two of the most misunderstood forms of folk magic. People often think of them as inherently evil or, in the case of Brujeria, simply another term for witchcraft. However, this isn't the case. In this chapter, we'll look at these practices in detail to understand what sets them apart from other folk magic traditions.

Brujeria and Curanderismo are two of the most misunderstood forms of folk magic.
https://www.pexels.com/photo/blindfolded-woman-with-a-candle-5435274/

Understanding Brujeria

Brujeria is the Spanish word for "witchcraft." However, it means more than simply witchcraft in another language. Instead, Brujeria is an indigenous system of folk magic with a long history, mainly practiced in Latin America and the Caribbean. The earliest known recording of this practice appeared in the 1500s. However, most brujas and brujos believe that the practice originates from the Aztec and Mayan civilizations of Mesoamerica.

As a result of slavery, Brujeria was forced to become a hidden practice. It was punished by Catholic land and enslavers who imposed their own views and beliefs. At the same time, transporting slaves around the Americas also led to the spread and development of Brujeria, as peoples from the continent came into contact with each other and shared their knowledge.

Although Brujeria is often denigrated as evil magic, in reality, it's the practice of magic - whether for good or evil. Brujas (female practitioners) and brujos (male practitioners) can practice both black and white magic. However, this depends on the individual practitioner and isn't a defining characteristic of Brujeria as a whole.

Gods in Brujeria

What sets Brujeria apart from many other folk magic traditions is the absence of a deity figure. Unlike many other indigenous practices like Santeria, Brujeria followers do not worship a particular god. Besides, contrary to most religious systems, there is no hierarchy of brujas and brujos.

It's essential to note that, due to the Catholicization of Latin America, Christianity is now deeply embedded in the practice of Brujeria. Many practitioners are also Christian, and many people hold Brujeria as a Christian system of folk magic. So, while Brujeria itself doesn't have any deity figure, this doesn't mean that practitioners do not worship a deity, and often, this deity is the Christian god.

Brujeria and Magic

As mentioned, brujas and brujos can be practitioners of both dark and light magic. They use a variety of magical techniques, including divination, spells, potions, herbalism, and more. When brujas and brujos are sought out for help, they usually prepare love potions, conduct divinatory magic, and perform charms and hexes.

As Brujeria flourished in parts of the world that were deeply Catholic, this led to a fear of Brujeria as being evil. At the same time, folk belief in brujas and brujos remained strong, and they were often sought out when all other solutions failed. This is especially true for healing rituals, as Brujeria practitioners are believed to both be able to inflict and heal curses caused by the "evil eye." So, when modern forms of healing have failed, Brujeria practitioners often seek to address curses that lie at the root of a person's illness.

Brujeria rituals are generally spontaneous and unplanned. Because no hierarchy exists in Brujeria, there are also no organized rituals. Each ritual that is performed is intensely personal to the practitioner. Similarly, building altars and summoning spirits is a personal experience that differs from one practitioner to the other. Due to the variety of spirits that can be called upon, it's challenging to imagine Brujeria ever becoming an institutionalized religion in the same way as Santeria.

Now, while rituals are a personal experience, brujas and brujos share certain similarities. Since Brujeria is not a standardized system of magic, it's an oral tradition of folk magic, and many oral Brujeria traditions share a similar origin. Many Brujeria practitioners also follow a number of other folk magic traditions, including Santeria and Vodou. They bring these belief systems to their practice of Brujeria, calling on Santeria Orishas and similar deities and entities, creating a hybrid magic tradition unique to them. They may also call on the recently deceased to help them with magic or to reveal secrets.

Some Brujeria practitioners, especially those who practice a combination of folk magic traditions, prefer not to be labeled as brujos and brujas but instead be called healers. For example, those who use energy magic may like to be called *energy healers*, while those using sound magic may prefer the title sound healers. Ultimately, each practitioner's preference is as personal as the practice of Brujeria itself.

While brujas and brujos may call on spirits, it is Brujeria practice never to question what is revealed to them by the spirits. It's believed that the spirits are merely there to show them what is meant to be shown, not to be questioned and forced to reveal secrets they aren't willing to reveal.

Modern Brujeria

Aside from magic and magic rituals, Brujeria practitioners also practice magic as a form of resistance. Many Brujeria practitioners see their magical tradition as a way of resisting colonization and reclaiming an indigenous practice that fell out of use due to pressure from the Catholic Church. For many practitioners, it served to reclaim an identity from which many had previously felt disconnected. This is especially true of Brujeria practitioners in the Latin American and Afro-Caribbean diaspora, who may not have the same connection to the land as native Latin American and Caribbean people.

At the same time, younger generations are starting to explore the world of Brujeria. This is because there are now far more brujas than brujos, and many women see Brujeria as a source of power that they may otherwise be lacking in a male-dominated world. Additionally, many people are becoming comfortable exploring family traditions, Brujeria, and magic. This is leading to more women becoming brujas, and it's once again common to find brujas and brujos in Latin American and Afro-Caribbean communities worldwide.

However, because Brujeria is an oral tradition, becoming a practitioner can be challenging. This is especially true if no one is there to instruct a new practitioner in their close family, as they must instead find an experienced guide in Brujeria.

Aside from rediscovering familial traditions of magic, what draws people to Brujeria is that it doesn't discriminate based on factors like age, ethnicity, or gender. While there are more brujas than brujos, this is simply a result of personal interest rather than oppression against male practitioners. Instead, Brujeria judges people on their abilities and the results they provide, making it a popular magical tradition for those looking to showcase and develop their powers.

Understanding Curanderismo

Curanderismo is a Latin American system of folk healing. It's found and practiced in many Latin American communities, including Mexico, Guatemala, Honduras, and Argentina. Curanderismo is often considered Mexican folk healing. However, this isn't the case. In Mexico, it's also known as "medicina del campo," or traditional folk medicine.

The history of Curanderismo is a long one. It traces back to various Mesoamerican civilizations, including the Olmecs, Aztecs, and Maya. It's essentially a combination and synthesis of several healing traditions found in these cultures, but other cultural and healing traditions and religions, including Roman Catholicism, have also influenced it.

As a result of cultural exchange and geographical proximity, Curanderismo also made its way to the United States. It was and remains most prominent in the country's southwest but is practiced nationwide. It was prevalent in indigenous communities, which had exchanges with Latin American peoples prior to Columbus' discovery in 1492.

Curanderas are healers who believe that disease is caused by a confluence of factors, not just physical or mental ones. Other influences can include environmental, spiritual, and social concerns. The goal of a curandera is to heal patients by helping them strike a balance between themselves and their surrounding environment.

There are many types of curanderas, depending on what type of healing they practice. Some include:

- Yerberos, or herbalists
- Hueseros, or bone and muscle healers
- Parteras, or midwives
- Oracionistas, or prayer healers
- Sobadors, or masseurs

In some practices, brujas and brujos may also be considered curanderas. This occurs when they use magic to treat illnesses of the soul or those caused by evil magic. In this position, they operate similarly to witch doctors.

Curanderismo is influenced by an amalgamation of different medical traditions. Aside from traditional Mesoamerican systems of healing, influences include African Santeria, the Greek theory of humor, Arabic healing traditions that help with the direction of psychic energy, and spiritualist traditions that help healers communicate with the spirits.

Curanderismo is also influenced by modern medical theories, such as germ theory. Many curanderas will advise patients with physical ailments to consult a modern allopathic doctor alongside their traditional treatment. This is because they believe modern medicine has its value and that curanderos don't have the answer to all ailments.

Gods in Curanderismo

Curanderismo can be considered a Catholic folk healing tradition to a certain extent. Many curanderas are Catholic and believe that the gift of healing is a gift from God. Several healing practices involve praying to God, and the training of curanderas involves prayer, religion, and learning to use both to help heal clients.

There is also the consideration that, for many curanderas, the decision to become a healer is less a conscious decision and more a "calling," similar to the calling to serve God in Catholicism. For that reason, the ability to practice Curanderismo is considered a healing gift from God.

Like in Brujeria, some curanderas bring other folk magic traditions to the practice of Curanderismo. This includes traditional Mesoamerican folk beliefs, African Santeria, and the belief in Orishas. Synthesis of these traditions creates a unique healing tradition for each curandera.

Curanderismo Healing

Curanderismo healing takes various forms, depending on the cause of the illness. Natural illnesses are treated with a combination of herbalism, prayer, and massage. However, even in the case of natural illnesses, curanderas work on all three levels the physical, spiritual, and mental. This involves:

- Treating the body with herbs, ritual healing practices, and conversation
- Treating the spirit with prayer and meditation. For some curanderas, this may also involve communication with spiritual beings like protectors, saints, and deities.
- Treating the mind with directional healing and mental focus

In Curanderismo, many illnesses are thought to be caused by intense emotions. These are "espanto" (scare), "bilis" (stress), and "susto" (fright). The event that caused the person to be startled typically involves a natural disaster, an accident, or a death in the family.

Some symptoms of susto are:

- Depression
- Insomnia

- Dreamless sleep
- Nervousness
- Diarrhea

Some symptoms of bilis are:

- Loss of appetite
- Irritability

Additionally, some illnesses are thought to be caused by mal aire or mal viento, meaning evil air or evil wind. These result from the movements of the air and can cause illnesses. Evil air can be hot or cold, and the illness can be caused by a movement from a hot space to a cooler space or vice versa.

Other causes of illnesses include dark Brujeria, when a curse is cast on a person, or when they encounter supernatural beings, including "espiritus" (spirits) and "duendes" (spirit creatures). Illnesses may also result from the "mal de ojo" (evil eye), an evil intent targeting a person, or a "mal projimo" (bad neighbor).

Lastly, there's also the case of soul loss. This may be the result of espanto or susto, or it may be an illness that affects a person independently of these ailments. Younger people are more prone to suffering from soul loss, and symptoms are similar to those experienced during susto and espanto.

Cases of physical and magical illnesses can be treated thanks to various "limpias," or purification rituals, in which specific objects and tools are used.

These can include:

- Eggs
- Holy water
- Herbs and spices
- Fruits (especially lemons)
- Flowers
- Incense
- Crystals
- Oils

- Pictures of saints
- Crucifixes and other religious objects
- Candles and incense
- Amulets
- Animal-based medicines (like snake oil and bufo toad medicine)

One of the best-known limpias is the temazcal ceremony, which is essentially the use of a sweat lodge. This ceremony is thought to remove impurities from a person's body and return them to the pure in-utero state.

Some limpias are relatively easy to perform and can be carried out by the individual rather than a curandera. By contrast, other limpias required a qualified practitioner to help lead the purification ceremony. Some limpias that you can perform on your own include:

Egg Cleanse

The egg cleanse is one of the most common limpias. It can be practiced by both professional brujas and curanderas, as well as individuals.

You'll need a fresh, clean, unmarked egg to perform an egg cleanse. The first step is to rinse it with a mix of salt water and lemon juice. If you are religious, you can reference the deity you follow while doing so (for example, Christians might make the sign of the cross over the egg or reference the Holy Trinity). When you have cleaned the egg, roll it over the part of your body that is hurt, injured, or aching. While doing so, ask the spirits to help heal your injuries by siphoning off the negative energy that's affecting your body into the egg.

After you've finished the healing portion of the limpia, the next step is to use the egg to divine your future. To do this, simply crack the egg open over a bowl and allow the yolk to fall out, discarding the white. Once the yolk has settled in the bowl, you can read it, similar to reading tea leaves. While this portion of the limpia is generally performed by an experienced curandera, there are some signs that are easily readable even by individuals. For example, a black yolk indicates bad luck and signifies that you should visit a bruja or curandera for more experienced help. Or, you can simply skip this step if you're not confident in your ability to read yolks.

Once the limpia is concluded, you can get rid of the egg and the negative energy it has absorbed by flushing all parts of it down the toilet. If you didn't use it to divine the future, you should first crack the egg before flushing it so that all the negative energy is released. After you flush it away, wash your toilet with salt and lemon juice to prevent any negative aura from lingering around your home.

Sweeping

This limpia is known as "barrida" in Spanish. You need three basic supplies for this one: a bundle of herbs, floral water, and a red string. Once you have the materials gathered, the first step is to bundle the herbs into a bouquet and tie them together with a portion of the red string. Wrap the remaining red string around your dominant hand (the one you write with). The red string should wrap around your palm at least twice so that it crisscrosses over the area.

Once it's ready, sprinkle floral water over the bouquet of herbs. If you're religious, you can also use holy water for this purpose. Stand up, holding the bundle of herbs that you just prepared, and focus on the intention of this limpia, which is to remove bad luck and negative energies from your body. You can also call on any deities, spirits, or gods you believe in while doing so. As you focus on your intentions, starting at the top of your head, use the bundle of herbs to "sweep" over your body.

The herbs sweeping over your body will eliminate all the negative energy from you. Once you're done with this step, dispose of the herbs in a bin outside your home. Remember to thoroughly clean your hands after you do so to clear away any lingering negative energies.

Some herbal medicines commonly used by curanderas as part of limpias include:

- Aloe vera
- Papaya
- Poultices
- Tobacco (for spiritual cleansing)
- Rosemary (for spiritual cleansing)

Curanderismo Today

Modern Curanderismo is practiced around the world, especially in Latin America and the United States. Several celebrity curanderas and curanderos are famous for their skills and abilities, such as Don Pedro Jaramillo, Teresa Urrea, and Niño Fidencio.

Modern curanderas also use social media to reach a new generation of people interested in traditional forms of healing. Because Curanderismo works in concert with modern medicine rather than against it, many people are willing to try it for chronic illnesses, particularly mental health issues.

Furthermore, Curanderismo is benefiting from the global popularity of alternative medicine. Several studies on the effects of Curanderismo are currently conducted, especially in treating mental health issues such as PTSD. Many traditional Curanderismo herbal medicines, such as aloe vera, are gaining popularity in modern medicine because of their curative properties.

Curanderas are easier than ever to find in Latin American communities worldwide. Many institutions offer Curanderismo training in Mexico and at the University of New Mexico.

Still, a great number of curanderas remain informally trained. Many traditional curanderas are trained in an oral tradition, from teacher to pupil. The institutionalization of Curanderismo is happening through formal training opportunities. However, it still remains incomplete, as many portions of the oral tradition of Curanderismo remain undocumented, existing only in the knowledge of individual practitioners.

Additionally, many traditional curanderas fear that Curanderismo is being appropriated and distorted by "curanderas" who do not know of the traditional practices. The conflict between these diverging forces will determine how Curanderismo is shaped and governed in the future.

Questions for Self-Reflection

Are you wondering if Curanderismo and Brujeria are the correct folk magic traditions for you to explore? If so, here are some questions you should ask yourself:

- Do I feel attracted to the traditions of Curanderismo and Brujeria?

- Do I have relatives in Latin America? Do I have Afro-Caribbean or Native American ancestors who may have learned and practiced these traditions?

- Do I feel drawn to heal other people?

- Have I ever experienced mal de ojo or mal aire? Have I felt these conditions in other people?

- Am I interested in personal forms of folk magic rather than systemized ones?

- Am I interested in attending a course that teaches Curanderismo?

Chapter 4: Scottish Witchcraft

According to the standard view, witchcraft is a type of magic where both male and female witches use supernatural powers to practice spells and charms for selfish or evil purposes. In medieval Europe, witches were hunted and persecuted, as witchcraft was regarded as a force for evil. For that reason, Scottish people couldn't use the terms witchcraft or witches as freely as they do today. In Scotland, a male witch was called "buidseach," and a female witch was called "bana-bhuidseach." These denominations were widely used during the 16th century when witches sought to protect their secret identities. Scottish witches at the time used magic and supernatural powers for self-gain, and their magic was often harmful to their community, which goes against what folk magic represents. Unless there was war, it was unwise for witches to practice evil magic as it turned their communities against them.

According to the common view, witchcraft is a type of magic where witches, both male, and female, use supernatural powers to practice spells and charms for selfish or evil purposes.
https://www.pexels.com/photo/an-old-book-and-candles-on-wooden-table-with-glass-bottles-7978061/

In Scottish folklore, the term *witch* is often associated with self-serving acts. They didn't help their community, which at the time was frowned upon as most people worked to help others and used their magic to provide services for their town folk. Scottish witchcraft included many types of practitioners, but the most significant ones were the wise men and women who were referred to as "bean/fear fease." While these individuals were considered witches, they never regarded themselves as such because their magic was a force for good rather than evil. Their community noticed what these folks were doing for them and understood their magic was different from that of witches. During the witchcraft trials in Scotland, the people asked the court to spare wise men and women. They held these wise folk in high regard because their magic wasn't self-serving. However, history has often been unkind to witches and anyone who practiced magic, forgetting that some good folk used their powers for good and in the service of others.

The wise folk in Scotland helped protect their communities against the forces of evil. In order to practice this type of magic, they had to be blessed by Daoine Sith, who were supernatural beings. Unlike other charmers or healers, these individuals were specialists who could communicate with a world beyond our physical one. The Daoine Sith bestowed wise men and women with a gift that enabled them to perform tasks that helped their communities. These tasks included predicting someone's death, finding lost or stolen objects, healing people from curses, and prescribing remedies for ailments.

The wise men and women were different from the cunning folks. Notably, charmers and healers didn't get their gift from the Sith, nor could they communicate with them, while the cunning folks got their knowledge from occult books. Scottish men and women who connected with the Sith could pass this gift to their children. Scottish clans also served as Sith helpers, making it easy to communicate with them and use their knowledge to practice magic.

History and Culture of Scottish Witchcraft

The history of Scottish witchcraft isn't pleasant, to say the least. Witches were essentially blamed for all the country's ills. People feared them, and as a result, the Scottish Parliament passed an act in 1563 that made witchcraft a capital offense. This act notably aimed to prevent the spread of pagan beliefs and the worship of saints and prohibit magic practitioners like the cunning folk from practicing. Witches struggled during these harsh times, not only because of the law but because people were hunting them as well. Moreover, healers and cunning folk were also the targets of this persecution. Cunning folk and healers were a force of good, using their magic to help the sick and protect them from evil spirits. It was a dark time in Scotland when all witchcraft practitioners were considered a danger, even those who helped their community.

Witches were blamed for any misfortune that occurred in the community. For example, in 1591, King James VI was at sea when a storm hit and almost sank his ship. About seventy witches were blamed for attempting to commit regicide. Any regular incident was considered a curse by witches, including when a child got sick or died prematurely, when crops didn't grow, or when cattle died. However, things changed in 1736 when the Parliament repealed the act, and witchcraft was no longer deemed a capital offense.

Nowadays, people still practice witchcraft in Scotland, and there aren't as many misconceptions about witches as before. People now know that images of witches flying on broomsticks or making spells over a cauldron are nothing but stereotypes. Most of the crimes witches were accused of back then weren't as serious as people made them out to be. In reality, many of these witches were helpful individuals who contributed to their communities.

Religion

Not much is known about religion in Scotland before the arrival of Christianity. However, historians believe its inhabitants were polytheists, like the Celts, who worshiped various deities and spirits. Pagans and the worship of deities influenced many branches of witchcraft. Scottish witchcraft is also syncretic, meaning it drew influences from several cultures and religions from all over the world, including Islam, Christianity, and Judaism.

Beliefs, Concepts, and Tradition

The Scottish people believed in supernatural beings and powers. These beliefs have been evident in Irish folklore for centuries. The Sith also had a great influence on Scottish witchcraft. "Sith" comes from the word Síd, whose various meanings include hill, goodwill, peace, and truce. These beings were believed to be fairies. Of note, various beliefs state that fairies are the spirits of the ancestors. The Scottish people believed that their ancestors lived in the otherworld. In fact, back then, they believed that the first person buried in a graveyard would later become its guardian. This is further proof that they believed the Sith were their dead ancestors.

Scottish practitioners communicated with the Sith to help with their magic. Some were clairvoyants, meaning they had the gift of second sight and could communicate with the other world. Those who didn't have this gift often used divination or made an offering. The Sith represented the dead that resided in the otherworld. Keeping a peaceful relationship with the Sith was essential to keeping the community safe. If one doesn't give them proper attention, they could inflict severe harm on local communities.

The fairy faith was also prominent among the common people. Some of their festivals, like Beltane (Bealltainn) and Samhain (Samhuinn), don't focus on worshiping a god or a goddess. Fairies have always been of the utmost significance, and these celebrations were focused on honoring their ancestors.

There are claims that some witches also believed in the devil, which was evident during the witches' trial in Scotland as some claimed to have renounced their baptism and made a deal with the devil. However, there are no records that prove witches worshiped the devil. It's believed that the church spread these rumors to scare people of witches and justify hunting them.

Scottish magic is also animistic and believes that everything, whether animate or inanimate, has a soul.

The people's belief system at the time focused on fairies, supernatural beings, spirits, the Devil, and religion.

Deities and Mythical Beings

Nicnevin

While the name Nicnevin may sound unfamiliar to most people, it's one that had a great impact on Scottish folklore and witchcraft. Nicnevin is a goddess and the queen of the fairies. Her name comes from Gaelic, meaning "daughter of frenzy." This etymology indicates that she could be linked to Neamhan, the Irish goddess of battle who made soldiers agitated during wars. Another theory, albeit not a very popular one, claims that Neamh means "heaven." It's also believed that this queen of the fairies comes from "Nic Noahm," which means "daughter of the Saint." While no one knows who this Saint may be, there are claims it was Saint Brigid.

Nicnevin's physical appearance isn't described in many literary works. However, in the few times her looks were mentioned, she was depicted as a woman wearing a long gray mantle. She also holds a powerful wand that gives her power over sea and land and allows her to alter her surroundings.

Nicnevin is also often compared to Cailleach – the goddess of winter and a prominent deity in Scottish and Irish mythology. Her name means "hag" or "the old woman." She is also known as Gyre-Carline – "Gyre" is Norse for greedy, and "Carline" is ancient Scottish that translates to "old woman." Another similarity between the two goddesses is that they rule over the sea and land and can transform their surroundings. Another theory regarding Nicnevin's origin that links her to Cailleach is that the "Nc" in her name means "the daughter of," while Nevis refers to Ben Nevis (mountain of snow). Ben Nevis is believed to be Cailleach's home.

Nicnevin is mentioned in various literary works and folklore. She was considered a scary figure that parents often used to scare children who misbehaved. She was also considered the queen of witches and a witch herself, which is why she is a prominent figure in Scottish witchcraft. Her first mention in Scottish literature was in a 16th-century poem by Alexander Montgomerie, where she appeared with her "nymphs," a term that describes female fairies. In the poem, we're told that she had charms, which refer to spells, implying that she was skilled in enchantment and divination. It also teaches us that she was riding with a fairy king, indicating that she may have been a fairy queen.

In Scotland, people consider Nicnevin a witch, even calling her "Grandmother Witch." During the witch trials, prosecutors often connected the witches to Nicnevin. Those who bore her name or a similar one were prosecuted. Various claims about Nicnevin linked her to Scottish witchcraft. Some say she was a regular human witch who was executed during the witch trials. Other claims attribute her to a more prominent role, namely, queen of witches.

Although much about Nicnevin is lost in history, all the information about her links her to fairies and witches. For that reason, Scottish witchcraft is inherently associated with the mythical figure of Nicnevin.

Cailleach

Also referred to as the "veiled one," Cailleach is the Celtic goddess of winter and winds and one of the oldest deities in Scottish mythology. Her name is a Scottish word that translates to "old woman." Cailleach is often depicted as an old woman wearing a veil and clothes decorated with skulls and having red teeth and pale skin. She had the ability to ride storms and shapeshift into an imposing bird. Considered both a destroyer and a creator, Cailleach was also referred to as the queen of the winter because she controlled its weather and duration. She was a significant figure in several countries in Europe as well.

Poets gave Cailleach various names in literary works and included her in several myths. She was called Buí, wife to Lugh, the god of justice, Biróg (who was a fairy), Digde, Burach, and Milucra. Due to her multiple names and the roles she played in mythology, scholars have debated whether Cailleach is a name or a title given to old women throughout history.

The old Gaelic "Cailleach phiseogach" means sorceress, and "Cailleach feasa" translates to *fortune teller*. For that reason, she is often referred to as a witch. Cailleach was a healer who used her ability to see into the future and cure the sick. She had knowledge of herbs, which she used to diagnose and treat many ailments, including emotional trauma. She would conduct her healing work to cure individuals and help heal entire communities.

In various stories, Cailleach is described as a woman wearing an apron and holding a wooden staff. In others, she is either holding a wand or a hammer. There are even other accounts of her holding a walking stick or a shillelagh. Invariably, whatever she was holding was made of the wood of a blackthorn tree, which has always been linked to witches and their powers. It's believed that the common depictions of witches as old women wearing black clothes and carrying a broom are influenced by the image of Cailleach.

Traits and Types of Scottish Witchcraft

Saining is a popular type of magic in Scottish culture, one with which many practitioners are familiar. It's an act of purification that resembles smudging but with slight differences. Practitioners would practice saining to get rid of negative spirits. It's usually done on people, animals, objects, and places. Since Scottish magic is animistic, the process of saining focuses on communicating with the spirit found inside each person and asking it to banish any negativity or evil spirits.

Various types of saining practices exist, each involving its own tool. The practice usually takes place in a community, over land, or around a specific person. Saining is most commonly conducted during festivals like Samhain and Beltane when people light huge fires to purify the entire town. Midwives would also purify newborns and their mothers. They do so by lighting a pine candle and spinning it around the bed three times while chanting a specific charm.

A characteristic trait of Scottish magic is its focus on healing spells and charms. When someone is ill, the wise man or woman would say a few words over the sick person and the water they were about to drink. This works on animals as well.

Another type of witchcraft involves granting protection for homes, animals, and people. To protect a person or animal from danger, the wise man or woman would utter a few healing words over the person's head, then place strings around their neck and leave them for a whole night. The wise folks would also tie a stone around a cow's tail while uttering a few words to protect them from evil.

For bacterial eye infections, the wise folk would leave the end of a stick in the fire, then take it out and point it at the infected eye. They would then spin the stick in circles while repeating a charm nine times.

Divinatory Practices

A few centuries ago, life was tough for Scottish Highlanders. As superstitious folk, witches, spirits, and fairies played a major role in their lives. Seeing as they blamed the witches for everything, any misfortune that would befall them was the witches' or fairies' fault. It was a time of uncertainty for the Scottish people. So, to protect themselves and their families, they turned to divination, often seeking the help of a seer or a person with second sight.

There are various types of divination practices, one of the oldest being speal bone divination. Practitioners would use an animal's shoulder blade after boiling it to foretell the future. They would also read tea leaves, one of the most popular divination practices in Scotland and around the world.

Many people prefer to practice divination on Samhain, which is the equivalent of modern Halloween. On Samhain, the veil between the world of the living and that of the dead is at its thinnest, meaning spirits and fairies can easily travel through it. Practitioners and wise folk would take advantage of this occasion to practice divination and seek advice and answers from the spirits. The festival of Beltane and Imbolc were also occasions for practicing divination. Scottish people believed no other days in the year were as powerful as the days of these festivals, which is why they presented the perfect opportunity to connect with the spirits and seek their wisdom.

Questions for Self-Reflection

- Do I have any Scottish ancestors?
- Have I ever had a dream of a Scottish deity or fairy?
- Do I agree with the beliefs of Scottish witchcraft?
- Do I feel attracted to Scottish witchcraft?
- How do I feel about the witch trials and how witches were treated back then?
- Do I want to learn more about Scottish witchcraft culture and history?
- What do I plan to do now with the information I have just learned?

Scottish witchcraft plays a prominent role in the world of magic. Although witches were persecuted and witchcraft was deemed a crime, many of the offenses they were accused of were unfounded. In reality, they were wise men, women, and cunning folk who helped their community and showed the world that magic could do more good than harm.

Chapter 5: Druidry and Celtic Magic

In the past few years, interest in spirituality has been on the rise. While many people have turned to Christianity or other well-established religions, others are exploring different ways of connecting with nature and finding peace within themselves. One of these paths is Celtic magic and Druidry. With over 7 million people identifying as Pagans, Heathens, Wiccans, or with other Neo-Pagan practices, the influence of these religions is growing worldwide. Druidry, in particular, is one such practice that has gained more attention recently. It's a religious tradition with ancient roots that has experienced a revival in recent years, particularly in Europe. Whether you're new to this faith and want to learn more about it or simply interested in exploring a new topic, this chapter will outline everything you need to know about Druidry and its followers today.

Druidry is a nature-based spiritual practice rooted in the ancient Indo-European culture that once spanned much of Europe and the British Isles.

https://www.pexels.com/photo/photo-of-the-stonehenge-historical-landmark-in-england-2497299/

Who Were the Druids?

The Druids were a group of people living in Europe and the British Isles thousands of years ago (3rd century BCE). According to historians, the Druidic religion was practiced in many parts of Europe, including Wales, Ireland, Scotland, France, and Spain. You can even find records of people practicing Druidry in modern times. The Druids studied and passed down knowledge about nature and natural laws. It's believed that they were also responsible for learning about ancient knowledge like language, culture, and philosophy. The Druids were also political leaders in Celtic societies. They're frequently featured in ancient historical accounts and folktales, which is why many people know about them today. They likely advised rulers on natural phenomena and served as judges. While there's no homogenous set of beliefs that all Druids follow, there are some common Druidic beliefs. One of these is a reverence for nature. Another is an interest in studying language, culture, and philosophy. Druids were also responsible for memorizing large amounts of lore, which they passed down orally.

The History of the Druids

Druidry is a nature-based spiritual practice rooted in the ancient Indo-European culture that once spanned much of Europe and the British Isles. The Druids were priests in the ancient Celtic society, where they studied and passed down lore about nature and natural laws. This likely included instructions for what we now call spirituality and philosophy. Many Druids were also political leaders in Celtic society, which is why they were largely featured in ancient historical accounts and folktales. Although historians disagree on how exactly Druidry and Celtic society operated, most agree that Druids were respected for their knowledge about the world, particularly the natural world.

There is very little historical evidence about the Druids and those who followed their beliefs. What is clear, however, is that the Druids were the religious leaders of the ancient Celtic people. The Druids held the world as a place of magic and mystery. According to them, all creation was alive with spirits and energies. The Druids followed a path of nature worship, meaning they revered and honored the beauty and power of nature. The Druids believed that all natural things had spirits or "souls," just like humans. They also had a deep and powerful connection to the creative energy of nature, which they called "the Force," and they believed that it flowed through all things, even rocks, trees, and plants. This creative energy was also present in humans. The Druids believed that everyone had the ability to harness and channel this creative force.

Druid Influences

Many people who practice Druidry today blend it with other magical or religious paths. Druidry has Celtic roots, but there are many other influences as well. These include:

- **Wicca and Witchcraft:** The most common path people blend Druidry with is Wicca or Witchcraft. Both of these paths include a belief in the power of the Force and a practice of channeling and working with it.

- **Magical herbs:** Celtic druids were also known for their knowledge of the magical herbs and plants found on their land. These herbs were thought to hold special powers and energies that could be used in various spells and rituals.

- **The elements:** Druidry is also often blended with the practice of working with the "elements." This belief holds that the natural world comprises four elements: fire, water, earth, and air.

Beliefs and Concepts

Like many other faiths, there isn't a single "Druid belief" or set of beliefs to which all Druids adhere. While they tend to share certain views, Druids interpret these ideas in different ways. The most commonly shared Druid belief is a reverence for nature. Druids believe that all of nature is sacred and interconnected in a web of life, including humans.

The Druids believed that everything in nature has a soul or spirit, including rocks, trees, plants, rivers, and lakes. There are no "ordinary" or "mundane" things or creatures in the world. To them, all is sacred and magical. Everything is connected and interdependent. The trees are connected to the mountains, the mountains are connected to the rivers, and so on. Everything is also connected to humans. It is our job to "listen" to nature and learn from it. The Druids believed that everything in the world holds a special creative energy, and anyone who is willing has the ability to channel and harness this force.

The Druids used this creative energy in their healing, spells, and in their everyday lives. One of the most important tools for Druids was the wheel of the year, a calendar that marks important holy days in the year. The wheel of the year is split into 8 seasons, with each season lasting about two months. The seasons of the year are related to the cycle of nature and the plants growing and dying.

Key Practices of Druidism

Druids believe that nature is full of magic. It's a basic belief in Druidry that everything in nature is magical and that each person can access this magic through their connection to nature. For that reason, many Druids refer to their spiritual practice as "sorcery" instead of "magic." Druids practice a form of magic based on their connection to nature. They use plants, herbs, crystals, and other natural elements to connect with the spirits of the natural world. The Druidic concept of magic is based on the world as a living, breathing thing instead of a lifeless, impersonal machine. Rather than a mechanical system of cause and effect, it's a creative process that is constantly transforming and evolving. Druids believe everything is connected and the entire world is one organism. This allowed them to leverage the power of plants, animals, stones, and other natural elements to create magic that helped them achieve their spiritual goals.

Who Can Practice Druidry?

Anyone can practice Celtic magic and Druidry, regardless of age, gender, or religion. In fact, this path has been followed by people from all walks of life for millennia. It's a great way to connect with nature, find peace and order in your life, and learn more about yourself in the process. If you want to learn about Celtic magic and Druidry in greater detail, you'll find plenty of dedicated articles and books on the topic. Finding others who are interested in this particular path will also help you grow your knowledge, share ideas, and practice together.

The Ancient and Magical Art of Druidism: What Did Druids Use for Divination and Spells?

Delving a little deeper into the world of druids and their practices, you'll discover a lot more fascinating things about this mysterious group. They were a highly respected group with many followers. Today, many people follow the ancient ways of the Druids and incorporate their practices into daily life. The spells, rituals, and beliefs are not exclusive to any group but can be found across several cultures worldwide.

Much of what we know about the Druids has come from the writings of Roman and Greek historians, who weren't exactly unbiased sources. These accounts, which describe the Druids as a mysterious order of priests and natural philosophers, are filled with exaggerations and half-truths. A complete picture of what life was like for pre-Christian Celtic people is still unclear. However, there are things we do know for certain. The Celts believed in many spirits that inhabited their world. They had several gods and goddesses, each with their own strengths and weaknesses. And like many other folks, they practiced this magical art through spells and divination methods.

Druid Divination Tools and Practices

Before we delve into Druid spells and divination practices, it's helpful to understand the core beliefs that governed Celtic magical practices. First and foremost, people back in the Iron Age (the period in which the Celts lived) believed that everything in the world contained some kind of spirit. In Gaelic, these spirits were called "sidh." A sidh could inhabit anything - plants, trees, lakes, rocks, and even minerals. The Celts often placed offerings at these spots or asked the sidh for guidance. In parallel, the Celts used various divination methods to communicate with the spirits. Perhaps the most common way was through the use of augury (reading omens). They would observe nature and interpret what the spirits were telling them through the movement of birds and flight of insects, the motion of water, or the entrails of animals.

Druid Rituals and Ceremonies

Traditionally, Druids also performed rituals and ceremonies with the goal of influencing the world. One of the most common rituals was called "mutation," whose intent was to transform one thing into another. An example of a mutation ritual is the transformation of a caterpillar into a butterfly. Over time, the practicing Druid would watch the caterpillar carefully as it transformed into a butterfly. After careful observation, they would try to imitate the caterpillar's transformation in their ritual. This ritual was designed to transfer the butterfly's powers to the Druid. Another common ritual was called "immolation." This ritual was a form of sacrifice, often involving the killing or burning of animals. Immolation rituals were performed to appease the gods. If the Celts wanted rain or a bountiful harvest, they would conduct a rain or harvest ritual. If there was a plague or disease, they would perform a ritual to appease the gods and ask them to lift the plague.

Divination and Spells

While it's impossible to know precisely what kinds of spells the Druids used, we can make some educated guesses based on ancient stories. One of the most well-known accounts from the Celtic tradition is that of the Salmon of Knowledge. In this story, a young man named Finn McCool is tasked with finding wisdom and knowledge. As part of this journey, he set off to find a salmon that would leap out of a pool, eat his thumb, and then die. Finn waited for hours for the salmon to jump out. Then, suddenly, a salmon leaped out and ate his thumb. He hurried back to the pool, caught the salmon, and put it on a rock to die. When the young man returned to the rock to retrieve the dead salmon, he found it had turned into an old man. The old man revealed he was an ancient Druid who'd been trapped in the salmon's body for many years. The Salmon of Knowledge was one of the most popular spells used by the Druids.

Gods and Goddesses

A shared characteristic of ancient cultures is that they had a pantheon of gods and goddesses, and the Celts were no exception. While the Celts believed in many gods, two were more prominent than others. The first was Lug (Lugh), the god of the sun. He was associated with the harvest and growing season and was said to be a god of poetry and inspiration.

The other prominent deity was Nemain, the goddess of war and death. Nemain was known for her fury in battle. She was particularly important to the Gauls, the Celtic people who fought against the Romans.

Basics of Druid Magic and Divination Today

No single definition could pay proper justice to the Druids' magic and divination methods. Each person who practices these arts adopts the Druidic way of life in their own personal way. Since Druid magic is rooted in nature and draws its power from the earth, the practice is inherently connected to the environment, taking inspiration from the elements of nature. Druids believed everything in nature held a connection with the universe and the divine. They used their surroundings to enhance their Druidic spells and castings by finding materials found nearby. For example, they would use natural items with healing properties, such as coneflowers and lavender, to cast a spell for healing.

Modern Druidry

Unfortunately, there's no detailed guidebook on how to become a Druid. You must decide to walk this path and follow the guidance of your inner Druid. It may take a few years, or even longer, before you fully understand your Druid path. By remaining faithful and practicing, you'll eventually get there.

It's important to note that many different branches of Druidism exist, although most of them have more in common than not. Still, there are variations in practices and interpretations of Druid beliefs. The types of Druidism range from ancient Druid groups such as the Order of Bards, Ovates, and Druids (OBOD), the Ancient Order of Druids (AOD), to Neo-Druidism practice such as Hedge Druids (those who practice alone) and Grove Druids (those who practice within a small group).

Hedge Druids

Hedge Druids essentially combine Druidry and witchcraft. This term often refers to people outside of traditional lines of power and knowledge. They focus on balancing the elements, using nature to help achieve goals. They seek to connect with their environment, commune with spirits, and use their power for good. Here, the word "hedge" refers to the way they combine traditional magic and herbalism with modern environmentalism. They believe our relationship with the natural world is key to bringing about positive change in our lives. Without it, we risk falling prey to negative influences. A hedge Druid seeks balance between mind, body, spirit, and environment, working together as a whole system. This means they are open to all forms of wisdom, no matter where it comes from – whether it's spiritual or scientific. Ultimately, they hope to create harmony between humans and the Earth by learning how best to care for both.

Druid's Grove

A Druid grove is a small group of people who come together to celebrate and explore ancient Celtic spirituality and Druidism. It's a place where they connect with the natural world and each other. There are many benefits to joining a Druid grove, including meeting new and interesting people, learning more about Celtic culture and spirituality, and having a place to explore and grow as an individual. Luckily, you don't need to be an expert or have a lot of experience to join Druid grove. Many groves and groups are dedicated to newcomers, providing a safe place to ask questions. If you're interested in Druidism, you can find a group in your area or online. Ultimately, Druidism can be a great way to connect with nature, gain a deeper understanding of the world, and feel more fulfilled.

Is Druidry and Celtic Magic for You?

Druids are often viewed as nature lovers who practice a religion deeply rooted in the beauty and harmony of nature. While that is certainly true, the Druid tradition isn't limited to a love of nature. Druids are spiritual seekers who strive to connect with the natural world and with their own inner wisdom. They're also open to new ideas and ways of thinking. Druidism can be a great choice for people who want to learn about spirituality but aren't sure where to start or those who need guidance along the way. It may also be a good fit for people who feel disconnected from the surrounding world and wish to reconnect with nature. Druidism can help connect you with your own natural emotional state, so you can better understand yourself and others. This can be a powerful way to improve your relationships, increase self-awareness, and build confidence.

Due to the connection with nature, many people find Druidry and Celtic magic to be good alternatives for people to connect with the Earth and its natural cycles. Ask yourself the following questions to help you decide whether this practice is for you:

- Do I have an interest in plants, animals, or the earth itself?
- Do I feel connected to or concerned about the environment?
- Do I want to develop my intuition and awareness?
- Do I want to build a sense of spirituality?

Am I interested in the traditions and cultures of ancient belief systems?

In ancient cultures, druids were a privileged class of people who practiced the arts of nature and spirituality. These mystical men and women had extensive knowledge of the natural world, which they used in their rituals and practices. With their intimate connection to nature, Druids used various spells and divination methods to manipulate natural elements. From these practices, we can learn essential skills that can help us live happier, more fulfilled lives.

Chapter 6: Norse Paganism

The world's diversity of religious traditions is fascinating. Many of these faith systems have existed for thousands of years, and many continue to be practiced today. Some are well known, whereas others don't enjoy the same popularity. Each religion provides its followers with an insight into the world and our place in it. Even though Christianity is currently the largest religion in the world, other belief systems have been around for just as long, and even longer, although they don't receive as much attention as they once did. One such religious tradition is the Norse Paganism faith system.

Each religion provides its followers with an insight into the world and our place in it.
https://www.pexels.com/photo/a-person-covering-the-lighted-candle-he-is-holding-5435272/

Many people are intrigued by Norse Paganism but aren't exactly sure what it is or how it differs from other belief systems like Wicca or Druidism. In this chapter, we will explore everything you need to know about this lesser-known Scandinavian faith system, including what it is, its history, key practices, and famous figures.

What Is Norse Paganism?

Norse Paganism is an ancient religious faith system practiced by the Northern Germanic and Anglo-Saxons during the Viking Age (approximately 800-1100 CE). Norse paganism is sometimes referred to as Heathenism. The religion is based on an animistic worldview in which the universe is a giant organism where all creatures, planets, and even objects have souls. Norse pagans believe in a divine force known as the "Wyrd" or "Fate," which guides the universe and controls the fates of all beings.

The Norse were a Northern Germanic people who inhabited modern-day Scandinavia (Denmark, Norway, Sweden, Finland, and Iceland) during the Viking Age. Unfortunately, much of their history has been lost over time. Most of our current knowledge about the Norse tribes comes from a time after they converted to Christianity. While the details of Norse Paganism are not entirely clear, we do know that it's based on a pantheon of deities called the Aesir and Vanir. They include gods and goddesses, each representing different powers and characteristics to call upon during difficult times or for worship to give thanks. Some of the more prominent deities in Norse paganism include Odin, Freyr, Frigg, Thor, and Tyr.

The Norse Subgroup Asatru

The Norse people once thrived throughout much of Northern Europe and are known for their love of battle, bravery, and strong thirst for drinking. These brave, strong people had a culture so rich in tradition that it has survived to the present day, not just as fragments or antiquated stories but as an active religion with followers all over the world.

Asatru is the subgroup of Norse paganism followed by most contemporary practitioners of the religion. Asatru literally translates to "belief in the gods." It's an umbrella term that refers to many different types of Germanic paganism. Asatru began to emerge in the 20th century in reaction to the increasing influence of Christianity in Northern

Europe. The first Asatru group was founded in the 1970s. Today, Asatru is a recognized religion in several countries, with over 4,000 members in Iceland alone. While Asatru followers are largely united by their reverence for the Norse gods, certain other aspects of the religion are subject to debate. Some Asatru groups have adopted ideas from other Germanic pagan traditions, while others have remained faithful to the original Norse religion.

The History of Norse Paganism

Much of what we know about the early Norse faith comes from archaeological evidence, artifacts, and extant literature. As already mentioned, much of the information and practices of Norse Paganism were lost due to the conversion of the Norse people to Christianity. However, we do know that the Norse tribes were polytheistic, meaning that they believed in multiple deities. There are written sources regarding Norse Paganism dating back to the 10th century. These texts show that the Norse tribes were already converting to Christianity at this time and that Christianity was already widely practiced among the Norse people. Norse Paganism likely began to decline after the 11th century, and many of the Norse tribes likely converted to Christianity completely by the 12th or 13th century.

While there's a great deal of debate over the origins of the Norse people, the most widely accepted theory is that they migrated to Northern Europe from Southeastern Russia. The Norse were seafaring people who built large wooden longboats, called Viking ships, which enabled them to travel vast distances and establish settlements in areas such as Greenland, Canada, and even parts of Northern Africa. The Norse were also skilled craftsmen who produced beautiful artwork and intricate jewelry out of silver and gold. The Norse adhered to an animistic religion known as Norse Paganism. This religion was based on the belief that the universe was an organic organism that was created and sustained by a divine power known as the Wyrd. The Norse believed that every person, animal, and even inanimate objects, like trees, had souls.

Norse Pagan Influences

While Norse paganism is an ancient religion, it's also an evolving faith that has been shaped by the cultures of the different peoples that have practiced it. For example, Viking explorers traveled as far as Greenland and North America, bringing Norse paganism with them. However, the Inuit people they encountered were so different from the Norse people that they quickly incorporated Inuit customs into the Norse faith. Similarly, Norse pagans who migrated to Anglo-Saxon regions like England and Scotland had to adapt their rituals and practices to suit the cultures they encountered in those places. Therefore, the Norse religion has greatly evolved over time, taking on new customs, rituals, and traditions.

Norse Pagan Beliefs

While there's no one definition of paganism, it can be broadly defined as a set of beliefs and practices centered around nature and the elements. At its core, paganism is a worldview that emphasizes the interconnectedness between all things. It views nature as a source of inspiration and wisdom and seeks to honor and care for it. This worldview is also often rooted in reverence for the supreme being(s) and that all creatures, including humans, will be reincarnated after death if the gods are properly honored.

Norse beliefs fall into either one of two groups - those that arose from the old religion and those that evolved from the Christianization of Scandinavia. The latter group takes the form of folkloric stories, whereas the first group is manifested through archaeological findings and artifacts. Both sets of beliefs attempt to answer several questions about life, death, and rebirth. This includes existentialist considerations, such as why there is suffering in the world, but also deals with more transcendent ideas, such as fate, predestination, and free will. How did we get here? Where did we come from? How did we end up on this planet? These are some of the most important questions we must answer in order to find meaning in life. We must understand our origin story to know where we came from. In that regard, Norse mythology provides an excellent basis to answer these questions.

Key Practices of Norse Paganism

There are various practices associated with Norse Paganism. While many of them are difficult to decipher due to the loss of records, we do know of certain rituals and observances associated with this faith system. The Norse had a unique set of beliefs that involved magic, runes, gods, and other mythological creatures. They also had complex rituals and ceremonies centered on death, rebirth, and nature. For example, some written records indicate that the Norse people performed human sacrifices as part of the worship of the deities. Many Norse Pagans also participated in seidr, which is a form of shamanic magic. In seidr, practitioners enter a trance-like state in order to connect with the spiritual realm, communicate with deities, and practice healing. There are also written accounts mentioning that the Norse people engaged in blót, a ritual of sacrifice and feasting in honor of the deities.

Why Should We Care about Norse Paganism?

Norse Paganism is a fascinating religion that offers a unique perspective on the world. This religious tradition is a reminder that there are different belief systems that are just as old as Christianity but don't receive as much attention. Norse Paganism is particularly important because it offers a glimpse into what our world was like before the rise of Christianity. It's a way for us to gain insight into how other people perceive the world and their place in it. Norse Paganism is also significant because it shows how difficult it would have been for people to convert to Christianity. The Norse people were dedicated to their religion, and it took centuries for Christianity to gain a foothold in Northern Europe.

The Norse Druids and Magic

The Norse are renowned for their daring raids and fearless exploration of new lands. Their traditions thrived in the harsh climate of Northern Europe, and they developed a strong sense of faith in the gods, who they believed watched over them at all times. They believed the natural world was full of magic and that certain people were blessed with special powers known as "visions." These druids, or "see-ers" as they were known, played an important part in Norse society and assisted the chieftain with his duties and provided advice on important decisions. The druids also used their magical powers to aid the warriors before battle.

They were a sophisticated and complex culture, with great variety from region to region. They had rich traditions, many of which we still don't fully understand today. Norse druids and magical runes are just one example. It's well-known that the Vikings had a deep respect for nature and its many wonders, as evidenced by their frequent expeditions into the wilderness for hunting and fishing. However, some of the Vikings' practices appear to be more than mere reverence toward nature. In fact, several accounts of rituals seem to have been based on magic, particularly involving the use of special words (or "runes") as a way to connect with the spirit world or harness divine energy. Let's explore these curious accounts and attempt to understand what they could have meant in practice.

Norse Runes

Runes are an alphabet used by many cultures throughout Northern Europe, including the Vikings. The German word "runen" actually means "mystery" or "secret," highlighting how mysterious these alphabets seemed to people, and still do, even today. Although the origin and development of runes are still largely unknown, we know they were used for various purposes. Most commonly, runes were carved onto stones as a form of writing. Other materials like wood and metal were also used for inscriptions. However, there's also evidence that runes were used for other purposes, such as magic, divination, and even healing.

Many great cultures have used runes for divination. Among them are the Anglo-Saxons, Celts, and even the Vikings. In fact, the tradition of using runes for divination is so strong that runes have become synonymous with fortune-telling in many modern languages.

Norse Pagan Magic

The term "Paganism" broadly describes a wide range of diverse religions and philosophies. It's typically used as an umbrella term to encompass modern Neopaganism and Wiccan religions but can also be used to refer to pre-Christian cultures such as the Celtic, Germanic, Slavic, or South Asian peoples. The definition of "Pagan" varies widely according to individuals and groups. Many Neopagans self-identify as Pagan by default, whereas others may not identify with any particular religion. Neopagans who identify as Pagan tend to be more interested in their spiritual side than in any particular set of practices or rituals. These people may engage in one or more of the following practices: meditation, yoga, natural medicine, divination (including tarot reading and runes), nature-based spirituality, or other types of spiritual practices.

There is a staggering number of books and videos on the subject of Pagan magic. However, as you explore this fascinating topic, several things must be kept in mind. Firstly, Pagan magic is not synonymous with

Wicca. While Wicca is a specific type of modern witchcraft that incorporates elements from nature worship and Celtic spirituality, Pagan magic is simply any form of magic that originates outside mainstream Christianity. Secondly, Pagan magic does not necessarily have to be white-washed. Many forms of Pagan magic out there incorporate certain aspects of African, Asian, Native American, or other cultures. Thirdly, while Norse magic can take many different forms, it all traces back to one core belief, the power of the individual to control their own destiny. By tapping into this power, you can harness the full potential of your body, mind, and spirit for positive change.

Norse Pagan Rituals and Ceremonies

Most of the evidence for Norse Paganism comes from archeological finds. Most of these items are what we call votive offerings, which are things that people would leave behind to show respect to a deity or ask for a favor. These range from small pieces of jewelry to larger items like furniture or statues.

There is also a lot of evidence in written sources. There is no consensus of opinion among scholars on when and how the religion was practiced, but there are a few things that seem to be consistent across all sources. Firstly, there are references to rituals that were used to honor specific deities and ask for their help. Secondly, there are references to runes and other magical symbols. Thirdly, there is a lot of talk about spirits that appear in dreams and other forms of communication with the spirit world.

Other types of evidence, mainly from ancient texts, suggest that Norse rituals involved casting spells for healing or protection, making offerings to gods and goddesses, or creating sacred spaces for the ceremony. Sacrifices were also common in Norse paganism. Sacrifices, called "blót," could take many forms, including offerings of food and drink, animal sacrifices, burning incense or candles, and setting an object on fire. The type of sacrifice depended on the purpose of the ritual. For example, if you want to heal someone, you might sacrifice food or drink to help nourish their body.

In Honor of the Gods and Goddesses

Several accounts describe rituals involving specific gods or goddesses. For example, there are reports that Vikings would perform a ritual before traveling at sea to honor the god Tyr and ask for his protection. Similarly, there's a story about a Viking who became sick and was advised to sacrifice to the god Frey to be healed.

There are several explanations for why Vikings performed rituals and used runes for magic. Some scholars suggest that they were simply trying to mimic what they believed the gods themselves had done. Others argue that they were attempting to influence their gods and draw their power. Finally, some claim that these rituals were designed to create a sense of community and comfort and connect people with each other.

How to Practice Norse Paganism

If you're intrigued by Norse Paganism and want to learn more about this ancient faith system, you can do a few things. First, you can read up on the Aesir deities and explore their stories. It's best to read secondary sources like books or online articles, as Viking-age texts are often complex and difficult to interpret. Second, you can explore the writings of modern practitioners of Norse Paganism to gain insight into how people practice the faith today. Finally, you can explore the archaeological evidence and other artifacts associated with the Norse people. This may help you better understand the people and the faith system. So, if you're interested in Norse Paganism, there's no time like the present to learn more about this fascinating religion.

Is Norse Paganism for You?

While some people are actively trying to revive ancient Pagan traditions and practices in today's world, for most people, this term is simply a catchall for any interest in religion or spirituality that isn't explicitly tied to Christianity. If you're unsure what you believe or looking for an inclusive, personal spiritual path, consider Norse paganism. There are many paths you can take, from the simplest forms of nature worship and gratitude practice all the way up to more complex ideas about the relationship between humans and their surroundings. As long as you respect your vision and work respectfully with others, you don't need to feel pressured to fit into a single mold. Ask yourself the following questions to help you decide if this practice is the right one for you:

- Am I looking for an inclusive faith system?
- Do I feel attracted to the concept of the runes?

- Do I want the freedom to choose which parts of the faith to practice?
- Am I willing to learn about the various gods and goddesses within this faith?
- Do I prefer the idea of spirituality over a specific religion?
- Am I interested in meditation and self-reflection?
- Does the idea of deity veneration appeal to me?

As you can see, the Norse were a complex people with a rich history and culture. However, we are only just beginning to understand them, and there's still much to learn about this fascinating civilization. As modern-day archaeologists keep digging up new discoveries, we are gaining new insights into the Vikings' history, culture, religion, and practices. Norse druids and magical runes are just one example of the many complex traditions that the Vikings had. Keep in mind, though, that Norse paganism is an ancient religion that has evolved over time. While these facts provide a solid foundation, they're not the last word on Norse paganism. As religion continues to change, new ideas will inform and enrich the faith, making it even stronger.

Chapter 7: Jewish Magic and the Kabbalah

With its diverse forms, Jewish mysticism is one of the most multifaceted religious traditions worldwide. The practice varies from moderate intellectual pursuits of understanding the Creator's world to intensive experimentation in non-religious activities. The former incorporates the traditional aspects of Judaism, including following the commandments of the Torah. While this form typically infuses Torah practices with mystical symbolism, the experimentative side relies on grounding activities to communicate with the Creator. Reading this chapter, you'll see how Kabbalah, the most widely known form of Jewish mysticism, combines both practices. You'll also discover how the traditional elements meet the mystical side in the Tree of Life and the Sefirot.

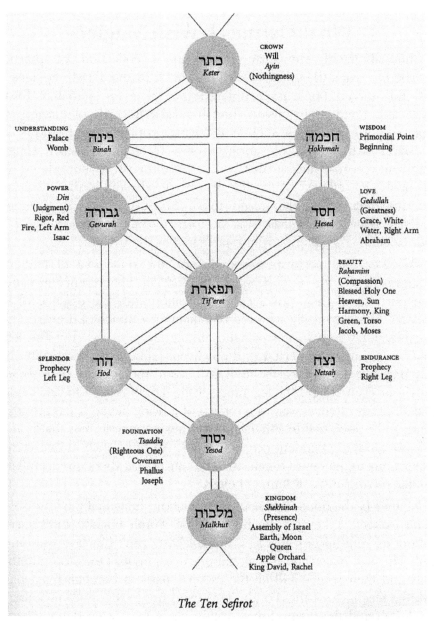

		CROWN
	כתר Keter	Will Ayin (Nothingness)

UNDERSTANDING Palace Womb — בינה Binah

WISDOM Primordial Point Beginning — חכמה Hokhmah

POWER Din (Judgment) Rigor, Red Fire, Left Arm Isaac — גבורה Gevurah

LOVE Gedullah (Greatness) Grace, White Water, Right Arm Abraham — חסד Hesed

תפארת Tif'eret

BEAUTY Rahamim (Compassion) Blessed Holy One Heaven, Sun Harmony, King Green, Torso Jacob, Moses

SPLENDOR Prophecy Left Leg — הוד Hod

ENDURANCE Prophecy Right Leg — נצח Netsah

FOUNDATION Tsaddiq (Righteous One) Covenant Phallus Joseph — יסוד Yesod

מלכות Malkhut

KINGDOM Shekhinah (Presence) Assembly of Israel Earth, Moon Queen Apple Orchard King David, Rachel

The Ten Sefirot

Jewish mysticism is one of the most multifaceted religious traditions worldwide.

What Defines Jewish Magic?

Traditional Jewish mysticism represents a collection of practices designed to reach the divine source presented by the Torah. Because of this, this sacred book is considered the pillar for authentic Jewish mysticism - and by extension, Jewish magic. Records of magical and supernatural experiences, such as receiving prophecies and visions, can be found in the works of various mystics throughout history. Certain historical records suggest that some of these were considered the potential "side effects" of the life of a mystic dealing in the occult and experimenting with folk magic tools. However, there's also clear evidence that Jewish magic was performed only for the purpose of understanding the natural order established by the Creator.

Whether they perform magic or not, the only goal of authentic mystics is to seek the understanding of God and his presence in nature. The purpose of their practices is unification with the essence of the Creator. This is typically achieved by obtaining as much of his wisdom as possible. They seek to uncover the infinite layers of the soul and learn how one's soul is connected to the heavenly spheres of spirituality. Not only that, but their practices often go beyond the concept of a physical body - or even behind the teachings of the Torah related to one's body. The Torah is often viewed as a replica of a living being. It has a body, a mind, and a soul, tied together and working as a whole. For that reason, they are always dependent on each other. An imbalance in one creates disharmony in the entire organism. The universe is also viewed similarly, just like the organism of human beings.

Neither body, mind, nor soul can function individually because they aren't isolated. Likewise, the body of the Torah (nigleh) can't survive without its soul (nistar), just as a human body can't function without its soul. Through magic and traditional practices, mystics seek to unite their body and their soul - and all the esoteric parts in between (halacha) - with the teachings of the Torah. This exposure to the inner meaning of the Torah and the divine forces within all of us is what defines Jewish magic and mystics, separating it from all other forms of mystical practices.

Unlike similar practices that seek a higher form of spiritual wisdom, Jewish magic is never used to confirm any preconceived notion. The answers mystics are known to pursue only serve to reveal the divine truth, even if it's different from what they were aware of. Mystics throughout history have used magic to discover what motivates human souls and what helps them grow spiritually. Those who reached an elevated state could glimpse the genuine and divine reality of the Creator – and their insights were verifiable. In fact, many of these insights are still being tested and proven today through modern Jewish magical practices.

Kabbalah and Jewish Magic

Kabbalah is the oldest and most notorious form of Jewish mysticism. Its roots are based on the writing of the Zohar, a collection of spiritual teachings and Jewish magical practices uncovered around the Middle Ages, originally written around the 2nd century. The English name of the Kabbalah stems from the word "cabal," meaning a "secret group" or "conspiracy," and was first used by medieval Christian writers. The same writers, rather than trying to fully understand the practices they were describing, made them forcefully fit into the doctrines of their own religion. As a result, there are still many misunderstandings surrounding Jewish mysticism, Kabbalah, and Jewish magic.

After its re-discovery around the 13th century, Kabbalah began to rise in popularity due to its connection to the Torah. It also contains a thorough description of the Sefirot, the only form of divine quality known to people. The revelation of this essence is a way to provide people with a better understanding of how the creation took place. After the 16th century, mystics began to delve into the experimental side of Kabbalah, combining its teachings with folk magic practices. This gave birth to a new form of Kabbalistic approach known today as contemporary Jewish magic.

Kabbalah means "tradition," signifying that Jewish magic tends to rely on conventional Jewish values and teachings. Due to this, it can't simply be a collection of personal insights and wisdom gained through mystical experiences. It's not even a system of magical practices practitioners developed due to their own cultural and religious backgrounds. It's a little bit of both. It also incorporates the elements of cosmology, ontology, and cosmology. As mentioned before, Kabbalah is based on the revelation of the Torah, not on speculative theories developed by people trying to find reasons for divine occurrences. It seeks to explore the relationship between the divine and its creations.

Mystics who delved into magic realized that the best way to test the hypothesis of Kabbalah is by experiencing them through magical practices. They considered the theories and prospective experiences, tested them, and after they managed to verify them, they labeled them as acceptable. Many of these mystics have immortalized their findings, providing reliable sources for working on the different aspects (essences), allowing future generations to continue these practices.

The Hebrew records of Kabbalistic practices also interpret the meaning of Kabbalah as "to receive and accept" and "tradition," yet another reason this school of thought became so popular. By accepting old traditions and combining them with Kaballalstic Jewish magic, they can better understand the divine as well as themselves.

The Tree of Life and the Archangels

According to Kabbalah, the Creator's energy cannot be portrayed in its elementary form because it is incomparable to anything humans will ever experience. The true essence of the Creator, known as "Ein Sof," has no boundaries and transcends everything and everyone. People and the universe itself interact with different energies by finding a point within a particular power that aligns with their energies. Ein Sof literally translates as "without end." This means this energy doesn't have an end or beginning people can grab onto and align themselves with. And this is why no one can interact with it directly. The sacred qualities, however, can be portrayed through their interaction with the universe through its offspring, the divine creations. The most famous illustration of the divine essence is the Ten Sefirot. The Sefirot also expresses how the Creator communicates with people – by showering his creative energy into the universe, which is picked up by the angels and further distributed to people. The interaction is exemplified in The Tree of Life, which has ten branches. Each branch represents a Sefirot, a form of the divine essence, and an Archangel that oversees the distribution of powers. The Archangels are beings born on the first day of creation and have since accumulated immense wisdom. For that reason, each of them has acquired a unique specialty. Their specialties are linked to the part of the divine essence they are charged to oversee. According to the Sefer Yetzirah (the Jewish book of creation), the Archangels are associated with the four natural elements of fire, water, air, and earth, as well as with the four divine elements, dominion, strength, mercy, and beauty.

The Tree of Life, also known as the flower or seed of life, has a female and a male side. The male energy is carried on the right side through the sephirah of wisdom, crown, eternity, kindness, and beauty. Whereas the female energy travels through the left side, enveloping the sephirah of splendor, understanding, kingship, foundation, and severity. The tree has a section called the "head," which contains the Sefirots' understanding, crown, and wisdom, all with the capacity to distribute the divine essence to the lower branches. These, in turn, are called the "body," and they illuminate the practical and emotional side of the divine.

While they often manifest themselves in human form, some claim that angels may also appear as spirits. Presumably, this is because people who experience interactions with them in the spiritual form are usually able to perceive only their spiritual energy and not their visual form. According to Kabbalah, angels live in a spiritual space where they can absorb the divine essence. This area is found between two of the Kabbalah worlds, Yetzirah (formation) and Beriah (creation). After delivering the divine message down below, angels help people elevate their energies into higher spiritual planes. Below, you'll see how each Sefirot is linked to the Archangels and what each Archangel's role is in people's lives.

Keter - Crown

The crown is overseen by the Archangel Metatron, who, as the angel of life, is the first to receive divine energy. He directs this essence towards the universe brought to life by the Creator, establishing a balance between the different parts of the universe. Metatron can help bring sacred spiritual power into people's lives. He is often revered by those wanting to obtain enlightenment and feels a connection to the divine, even though they can't interact with it directly.

Chokhmah - Wisdom

This sefirah is the dominion of the Archangel Raziel, the angel of mystery and secret. To help people obtain wisdom, Raziel leads them to the revelation of mysteries and truths they were aware of. Not only that, but Raziel also demonstrates to people how to use their newfound wisdom in practical ways. This Archangel is called on (through the Sefirot) by people wanting to reach their full potential or find the purpose the Creator bestowed upon them.

Binah - Understanding

Understanding is the sefirah ruled by the Archangel Tzaphkiel. As the angel of compassion and spiritual energy, Tzaphkiel is responsible for helping people understand the essence of the divine. He instructs people about the Creator, offering insights about his children (the people themselves and all living beings). Tzaphkiel is called on by people wanting to ensure their decisions align with their core identity.

Chesed - Mercy

This sefirah is illuminated by the Archangel Zadkiel, who, as the angel of mercy, ensures that God's mercy is equally distributed across the entire universe. He inspires people to find kindness towards others and show mercy, just as the Creator does with them. Zadkiel also helps people find peace through prayer by showing them that their prayers will be answered – as long as it's in their best interest.

Geburah - Strength

Led by the Archangel Chamuel, this sefirah is where the true essence of relationships stems from. Chamuel shows people that in order to build a strong relationship, they must be truthful to themselves and others. Having better relationships brings peace into people's lives. For this, the angel tests people's motivations in relationships, purifying them in the process, which ultimately allows them to have a better relationship with the divine.

Tiphareth - Beauty

The sefirah of beauty is the result of the Archangels Raphael and Michael working side by side. As the Creator's favorite angel, Michael helps express divine beauty to people and being the angel of healing, Raphael enables people to find and use beauty to heal themselves. By teaching people, the divine (true) meaning of beauty, this angelic duo allows people to reach a higher level of spiritual consciousness.

Netzach - Eternity

Archangel Haniel oversees eternity. This is the angel of joy, who distributes the divine essence of eternity by showing people they can rely on God. He doesn't expect people to change their emotions. Haniel provides insight that leads people to joy and happiness, regardless of their situations.

Hod - Glory

Also led by the dynamic duo of Michael and Raphael, Hod is the sefirah in which The Creator's glory is expressed. Because glory is beautiful, this branch is tied to beauty. The two Archangels ensure that the glory remains beautiful and victorious by eradicating sin from people's lives. They often help people reveal the meaning of glory in their own lives.

Yesod - Foundation

Foundation is the sefirah in which Gabriel, the angel of revelation, works. His dominion is communication and represents the foundation of people's lives, which is why he's entrusted with the foundation of the sacred tree. Gabriel is in charge of the messages people send to express their faith and the answers that allow them to rely on this faith.

Malkuth - Kingdom

This sefirah is ruled by Salphadon, the angel of prayer and music. This is another angel that helps people communicate with the divine. By allowing people to express their thoughts through other forms of communication, Salphadon facilitates the flow of information, nurturing the divine essence in everyone.

The Main Traits of Jewish Magical Practices

Nowadays, the practices of Jewish mysticism are open to personal interpretation. Some followers of the traditional customs rely only on the secret ancient writings found in the Zohar. Others take the mystical part of their practices more seriously, trying to connect the traditional elements with the magical. These practitioners often use Kabbalistic resources for prayers and magical acts alike. For example, they may have a book of traditional prayers and a book of shadows for spirituality-enhancing magic. Another group may refer only to folk magic, incorporating only a few Kabbalistic elements into their practice. This is usually tied to a specific essence (Sephirot) or energy mentioned in the Kabbalah. Even though they find it more worthwhile to follow the old beliefs, these practitioners often find solace and empowerment in the different divine energies.

Although Jewish magical practices have evolved through history, they remain parallel with the traditional teaching of the Torah. One of the most popular practices is visiting the ancestors' resting places, typically former practitioners (called sages) themselves. Because these sacred sites are believed to contain magical powers, they're often used for empowering spells, charms, and rituals. According to Jewish lore, these places hold elements of folk magic. For example, some are known for their exceptional healing powers, while others are said to help find love. Another practice that continues to this day is making magical amulets. Bracelets and other charms containing sacred inscriptions or symbols like hamsa are often used for healing, protection, warding off the evil eye, and enhancing magical powers.

Astrology is also incorporated into modern Jewish magical practices. The zodiac has served as a central motive for symbolism and divinatory practices. Contemporary practitioners often believe that the divine energy will give them insight into their present and future lives. This information can be found in one's mind or harnessed from the supernatural world made by the Creator. To reveal the former, mystics often use dream divination. However, they advise using prophetic dreams alongside other practices to obtain better results. A person's dreams can be influenced by good intentions, often offering an opportunity to receive spiritual messages. Yet they also are affected by malicious ones, which may lead to distorted prophecies.

While today, most practitioners prefer to invoke angels only, according to written historical evidence, both good and bad spirits were also called upon in the past. However, the same historical records show that very few mystics know how to interact with supernatural beings other than angels. This is why it's not advised to summon them, especially if you are a beginner just delving into this world.

In parallel, spellcasting is another magical act associated with modern Jewish magic. It remains unclear whether mystics used actual spells or incantations in ancient times. However, some consider that spoken magic (as spellcasting is often called) has been present since the beginning of time. Many practitioners believe that the act of creation was the spell cast upon the world. Spells can be used for constructive and destructive purposes, but many prefer using them for negative and truthful purposes only. Spellwork in Jewish magic typically revolves around invoking the divine energy and utilizing it to enrich one's practices and obtain the goal of revealing the truth.

Is Jewish Magic for You?

Because each person is naturally limited in their capacity to absorb the divine power of the Creator and the Torah, everyone must examine their own potential. However, having limited abilities doesn't mean you can't explore where they might take you. If you're wondering whether you have the ability to practice Jewish magic and, if yes, in what capacity, answering the following questions for yourself may help you discover whether this path is for you.

- Do I prefer enhancing my magic with divinatory practices, chants, and incantations?

- Do I use herbs or plants for healing or other purposes?

- Do I invoke just angels for guidance, additional energy, and more, or call on spirits too?

- Do I make and use charms and talismans to empower your practice?

- Do I frequent or wish to visit sites known for being magical energetic sources for Jewish mystics?

If you answered most of the questions positively, you would feel the need to be inspired by the mystical energy of the Torah and Kabbalah. If most of your answers are negative, Jewish magic may not be the right choice for you. However, if your answers are roughly evenly split between the two, you may still have the capacity to become a mystic. Feel free to continue pursuing the practices you feel the calling for.

Chapter 8: Sacred Plants and Herbs

Herbs and plants have always been linked to magic and supernatural lore. For centuries, people have depended on them for their healing abilities. From superficial wounds to serious ailments, they have been a source of healing and comfort. They also play a huge role in the practice of folk magic as well. Seeing as many folk magic practitioners were healers, it makes sense that they incorporated these sacred herbs and plants into many of their healing spells. They also used them in other spells that helped improve their communities and provided solutions for many issues they faced at the time. Practitioners also turn to sacred plants and herbs to connect with the other world and supernatural beings.

Cinnamon is one of the oldest herbs in the world.
https://www.pexels.com/photo/cinnamon-sticks-71128/

Every magic tradition uses sacred plants and herbs. Each of them has a long and rich history in these traditions. For instance, most people associate mistletoe with Christmas decorations and kissing. What you may not know is that mistletoe predates Christmas and has had a great influence on magic for centuries, starting with the Druids' interest in this plant. The same goes for many of the herbs you have in your kitchen. You may think they only serve as spices to make your dish tasty or provide a remedy for common ailments. However, these herbs and plants are more powerful than they look, and you can benefit from their powers just like your ancestors did. In this chapter, we will focus on sacred plants and herbs and learn everything they have to offer.

Chamomile

You may already be familiar with chamomile tea, as it is often recommended for people who need to calm their nerves. Chamomile is a herb that is essentially a beautiful flower with white petals, which you can find in many gardens. This herb is often included in various spells and magical rituals. Chamomile has been a part of the magical world since ancient times. Ancient Egyptians were one of the first cultures to use it, but the English made it popular.

Magic Traditions

It's believed that chamomile was used in Norse Paganism as it was very popular among the Vikings. In fact, it is the plant of Asgard and was mentioned in some of their literary works as well. It is also associated with the Celtic goddess of fertility, Cernunnos. In American folk magic and Hoodoo, chamomile is a popular herb that brings good luck. Before gambling, players often wash their hands in chamomile tea to increase their chances of winning.

Spiritual Meaning

Chamomile is a symbol of positivity, and its flower symbolizes poise and humility. The flower has the ability to make your wishes come true. Many magic traditions have similar interpretations of chamomile, viewing it as an herb that brings good luck.

Magical Practices

Chamomile can cleanse spaces and protect against magical attacks. It is also considered a lucky charm. Practitioners use this herb in banishing rituals as well. Similar to other herbs, chamomile can drive away negative energy and evil spirits. It is also a very popular herb in candle magic. Practitioners also use it to counteract a spell that was cast against them. It has always been an essential ingredient in prosperity and blessing spells and is also used in other spells and rituals.

- Practitioners use chamomile in spells to attract peace, happiness, and love.
- Practitioners wash their hands with chamomile before practicing any spell to increase their chances of success.
- They use chamomile in ritual baths that often take place before performing any spells.
- Chamomile in ritual baths can also help release negative feelings like anger or pain and help one let go of an old lover.
- Burning chamomile can attract money into one's life.

Cinnamon

Cinnamon is one of the oldest herbs in the world. Its place of origin is Sri Lanka, but other cultures have been using it for centuries. For instance, the ancient Egyptians used cinnamon to mummify their dead. The first people to ever use cinnamon were the Chinese in 2800 BC. In ancient times and now still, cinnamon has been known for its healing properties.

Magic Traditions

As one of the oldest herbs around, cinnamon exists in multiple cultures and magic traditions. It's used in African spirituality to protect people and homes from evil magic. In Curanderismo, Mexican folks use it on the Day of the Dead festival to get rid of negative energy.

Spiritual Meaning

Cinnamon has fiery qualities because it's ruled by Mars and the Sun. For thousands of years, this ancient herb has been a symbol of spirituality, fertility, good health, protection, love, and good luck. Practitioners use cinnamon to bless their magical tools and the space before casting a spell. There is a mysterious connection between cinnamon and the human spirit. Burning this fiery herb can increase one's spiritual powers and enhance their psychic ability. In various magical practices, practitioners seem to value cinnamon mainly for its protective abilities.

Magical Practices

When it comes to love spells, there isn't a better herb to use than cinnamon. It's a powerful aphrodisiac and can stir up feelings of lust between lovers. This is why practitioners often include it in sex magic and love spells. They also use it to bring an old love back. Cinnamon also has protective qualities, which is why people incorporate it into practices that serve to protect from negative energies. Some spells can take longer than others before showing real results. Practitioners who want to speed up the process often use cinnamon to make spells work faster. Cinnamon is also a necessary ingredient in healing spells, spells that bring good luck and those that bring success. Practitioners also include cinnamon in various other practices.

- Burning cinnamon can purify the space.

- Cinnamon can be used as a good luck charm.

- Cinnamon can cleanse and purify your divination tools and charge them with clairvoyant energy. Simply put a cinnamon stick in your tools or runes bag or in your tarot card cloth.

- Practitioners include cinnamon in moon rituals and spells that bring joy and wealth into your life and provide protection.

- Drinking cinnamon beverages can increase practitioners' insight and assist them in divination.

- Practitioners include it in rituals that bring prosperity, success, or whatever a person desires.

- Practitioners use cinnamon in rituals that bring victory.

Frankincense

Frankincense is a type of plant that's considered a magical resin. It grows on trees and is associated with African cultures, among others. People all over the world have been using frankincense for centuries. Cultures that believe in reincarnation bathe newborn babies in frankincense oil to cleanse the baby from past lives' demons.

Magic Traditions

In Hoodoo and rootwork, practitioners use frankincense to bless their petitions. Frankincense has a potent vibrational energy, which is why Hoodoo practitioners often mix it with weaker herbs that could use a magical boost. In African tradition, the scent of frankincense is believed to have the ability to ward off evil spirits.

Spiritual Meaning

For centuries, practitioners have been using frankincense in spiritual rituals. This magical resin symbolizes righteousness and holiness. Various practices use frankincense for its protective qualities.

Magical Practice

Practitioners use frankincense to purify spaces, especially sacred ones. It's also known to bring good luck. They also use it in various spiritual rituals as it wards off negative energies. Healers have used frankincense in healing rituals and remedies since ancient times. Practitioners use frankincense in rituals that allow them to communicate with the other world or the spirits of their ancestors. It's believed that the fragrance of frankincense can get the spirits' attention so they can help the practitioners with their rituals. They also use it to invite good spirits.

Mistletoe

Most people are familiar with mistletoe as it's the famous Christmas decoration under which people often kiss. However, mistletoe is more than just an ornament. Various cultures throughout history have revered this plant. Mistletoe has several magical properties, and it's believed to be a good omen that can provide protection against witchcraft.

Magic Traditions

In Druidism, mistletoe played a big part in magical practices. It was also associated with the Celtic magic tradition, as the Druids highly revered it and considered it a sacred plant. The Druids believed that mistletoe was only powerful and effective when it was still growing on trees. However, it would lose all of its magic if it fell to the ground. For this reason, the Druids climbed on trees to harvest the plant. It's believed that the Druids were the first people to use mistletoe for decoration. To them, mistletoe wasn't an ordinary plant but one that had the ability to perform miracles. The Druids believed that the mistletoe was a symbol of life. They would watch how leaves often withered and fell off trees while the mistletoe thrived, maintaining its beautiful green color. The mistletoe remained vibrant in the middle of dying trees, which is why Druids saw it as a symbol of life and rebirth.

In Norse traditions, mistletoe was considered a good luck charm. In the Voodoo magic tradition, it's used to ward off evil spirits.

Spiritual Meaning

Mistletoe is a symbol of immortality, fertility, rebirth, magic, protection, femininity, peace, healing, and unification. The reason behind all these symbolic attributes is the powerful magic behind them. The plant has both female and male energies. It also symbolizes love, which is why it became a tradition for people to kiss under it. Voodoo, Druids, and Norse practices all had various interpretations of what this plant represented.

Magical Practices

Mistletoe is included in protection spells and ones that bring good luck. Practitioners also used it in spells to encourage forgiveness and attract love. It's commonly used in healing spells and protects against cold winters and various diseases. Other magic practices include:

- Protection against evil spirits, evil witches, and ghosts.

- Practitioners included it in remedies that could cure poison.

Mugwort

Mugwort is an old herb, but it's often used in modern magic practices.

Magic Traditions

Native Americans use mugwort to protect themselves against ghosts. It's also used in Shaman purification rituals.

Spiritual Meaning

Mugwort is associated with the goddess of the moon, Artemis, and is connected to lunar magic. Blending this herb with other herbs can provide a deeply spiritual experience.

Magical Practices

Practitioners use mugwort for various magic practices like smudging, spellwork, and as incense. Mugwort is also used in healing spells. In the past, people believed certain diseases were caused by the Fae (fairies) and that mugwort was the perfect herb to combat this type of disease. It's also used in divination practices to enhance the gift of prophecy. Mugwort is used in ritual baths to help people suffering from overactive dreams.

- Practitioners use mugwort as protection against psychic attacks

- They use it in divination like runes and reading cards

- Practitioners use mugwort to increase their psychic abilities
- Practitioners use mugwort in protective spells against evil spirits
- They use it in tea leaf reading
- They use it to cleanse divination tools
- They include it in incense rituals
- It's used to invite good spirits

Rosemary

Ancient practitioners valued rosemary highly, as they knew what this herb had to offer. At the time, rosemary was one of the most effective herbs for brain and memory issues. It isn't an exaggeration to say that every practitioner must always carry rosemary with them, as it can replace many herbs in spellwork. There is a misconception that since rosemary is used in witchcraft, it may not be safe to use in other types of magic. However, there's nothing harmful or evil about rosemary, and it's commonly used in various folk practices all over the world.

Magic Traditions

Several magic traditions around the world use rosemary as protection against evil witches and spirits. In Hoodoo magic, practitioners use rosemary for its protective properties. They believe it protects them against evil spirits and brings good fortune. It's also believed that this herb guarantees that a marriage will be long and happy and that both partners will remain faithful to each other. Rosemary is also popular among Druidry practices, where people use it to communicate with their ancestors and sharpen their minds. They also used it to attract fairies.

Spiritual Meaning

Rosemary is a symbol of spirituality and longevity. Back in the day, if rosemary was grown in someone's kitchen or garden, this meant that the lady of the house was the one in charge. According to mythology, this is the only way rosemary would flourish and grow. This herb has always been a symbol of memory and remembrance. For that reason, people often place it in graves to signify that they'll never forget their departed. Rosemary was also considered a symbol of love in ancient times. People believed that by placing the herb under their pillow, they would see the person they were meant to be with in a dream. Rosemary also symbolizes everlasting love, which is why many brides wear it on their wedding day.

It's also associated with faith, and many people use it when struggling with their beliefs. It can also prevent people from committing sins as it protects their souls and helps them resist temptation.

Different traditions have various interpretations of this herb. For instance, Hoodoo practitioners use it for its protective properties, while Druidry practitioners use it for divination and visionary work.

Magical Practices

Practitioners burn rosemary in front of their homes to protect them against thieves and anyone who wishes them harm. They also use it against bad omens and energies. It can also be an effective tool to cleanse the interior of homes. Rosemary is one of the most essential ingredients in spells to ward off evil spirits. Since it's a symbol of love, practitioners use it in love potions. Burning rosemary at home can drive away bad luck and attract good fortune. This herb is also a part of spells, rituals, and divination practices that provide healing and increase psychic abilities and spirituality. It's also used in other magical practices.

- Practitioners use rosemary in healing spells

- Rosemary is used in love potions to help people find true love

- Practitioners use it as a protection against bad events

- Rosemary is an essential ingredient in spells that invoke passion

- It's used in spells that can bring back an old love

Sage

Sage is one of the most popular herbs around. For thousands of years, people have used it to make herbal tea, as an ingredient in different recipes, and in various magical practices. Sage is known to be a healing plant, which is where its name comes from. The word sage is derived from "salvare," a Latin word that means "to heal."

Magic Traditions

Sage originates in European traditions. People would dry and smudge it and use it in cleansing ceremonies. European practitioners also used it to drive away evil spirits and protect their communities. They also used it as a good luck charm, and some people believed it could grant them immortality. Native American and Europeans use sage for its healing properties and as protection against evil. African traditions use African sage for cleansing, purification, and protection against evil spirits and negative energies. They also use it in divination and to communicate with their ancestors. Other cultures that use sage include the Inuit, Metis, and First Nations.

Spiritual Meaning

People all over the world have been using sage for its healing and spiritual properties for thousands of years. Ancient cultures used sage to protect them from evil spirits. They also considered sage to be a symbol of wisdom as people believed it had the power to grant them wisdom. The popularity of sage hasn't withered away. To this day, people believe in sage's protective abilities and use them to purify their homes of negative energies. In African traditions, people use African sage for the same spiritual practices and also as protection against ill-intended individuals.

Magical Practices

The most common practice for sage is smudging. Smudging is a Native American practice that works on cleansing a place, person, or group of people from negative energy. It's often done before spiritual work. You'll need a bundle of sage for this ritual. Light the tips with a match, let it burn for a few seconds, and then blow it out. Direct the smoke toward the person or space you want to cleanse. Practitioners also use sage for various other practices.

- Burning sage during funerals can help grieving families and create a bond between the mourners and the spirit of the deceased
- Scattering fresh or dried sage outdoors can bless the area
- Sage is the main ingredient in wisdom-granting spells
- Putting sage under a pillow can protect against nightmares
- Placing sage in your wallet can increase prosperity
- Practitioners use sage in spells that help a person get over someone or end an unhealthy infatuation
- Placing dry sage around a blue candle can calm the spirit

One of the most interesting things about sacred plants and herbs in folk magic is that they all protect against evil spirits. At the time, evil spirits were a real concern among communities. These herbs and plants served as protective tools and to put people's minds at ease. Nowadays, people have other fears and concerns besides evil spirits, like negative energies and people that want them harm. Using sacred herbs and plants can provide a solution to many of these issues.

We can't forget about their healing properties as well. Many of the folk magic practitioners were healers and cunning folks who used herbs and plants to diagnose diseases and heal their communities. In a later chapter, you'll learn various spells that you can perform using these sacred plants and herbs.

Chapter 9: Signs, Symbols, and Charms

This chapter enlists the most common charms used in the different practices mentioned in the previous chapters. First, you'll be presented with a list of symbols, and it will be up to you to decide which one you feel drawn to. Just look at them, and trust your gut to tell you which would be useful. In case you haven't yet determined which tradition aligns with your values, examining the symbols each practice is associated with will help you make a confident decision.

Here is the list of symbols to go over:

1. The Celtic knot

The Celtic knot.

Eugenio Hansen, OFS, CC BY-SA 4.0 <https://creativecommons.org/licenses/by-sa/4.0>, via Wikimedia Commons: https://commons.wikimedia.org/wiki/File:Triquetra-circle-interlaced-black.svg

2. The Celtic cross

The Celtic cross.
GabrielGGD, CC0, via Wikimedia Commons:
https://commons.wikimedia.org/wiki/File:Celtic_Crosses.svg

3. The Triquetra

The Triquetra.
https://commons.wikimedia.org/wiki/File:Triquetra-Vesica.svg

4. The five-fold symbol

The five-fold symbol.
https://commons.wikimedia.org/wiki/File:20-crossings-ornamental-knot.svg

5. The spiral

The spiral.
https://commons.wikimedia.org/wiki/File:Triple-Spiral-Symbol-heavystroked.svg

6. Ankh

Ankh.
Alexi Helligar, CC BY-SA 3.0 <https://creativecommons.org/licenses/by-sa/3.0>, via Wikimedia Commons: https://commons.wikimedia.org/wiki/File:Ankh_(SVG)_01.svg

7. Winged Sun

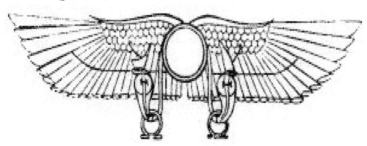

Winged Sun.
https://commons.wikimedia.org/wiki/File:Winged_sun_sharpe.png

8. Adinkra

Adinkra.

kasahorow from Openclipart, CC0, via Wikimedia Commons:
https://commons.wikimedia.org/wiki/File:Gye_Nyame_(Adinkra_Symbol).svg

9. The serpent

The serpent.

https://commons.wikimedia.org/wiki/File:Sea_Serpent_after_Owen_1741.png

10. The helm of Awe

The helm of Awe.
https://commons.wikimedia.org/wiki/File:Aegishjalmr.svg

11. The Hamsa

The Hamsa.
first version Fluff This W3C-unspecified vector image was created with Adobe Illustrator.new version from 2011 Perhelion This W3C-unspecified vector image was created with Inkscape ., CC BY 3.0 <https://creativecommons.org/licenses/by/3.0>, via Wikimedia Commons https://commons.wikimedia.org/wiki/File:WPVA-khamsa.svg

12. The Evil Eye

The Evil Eye.
https://commons.wikimedia.org/wiki/File:Evil_eye.svg

13. The Tree of Life

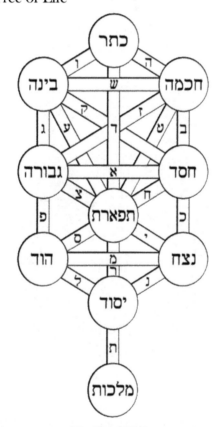

The Tree of Life.
https://commons.wikimedia.org/wiki/File:Tree_of_life_bahir_Hebrew.svg

14. Merkabah

Merkabah.
Joshua Free (creator of the concept), Ony Yahontov (creator of the file)., CC BY-SA 3.0 <https://creativecommons.org/licenses/by-sa/3.0>, via Wikimedia Commons: https://commons.wikimedia.org/wiki/File:Zuist_merkabah.svg

15. The Veves

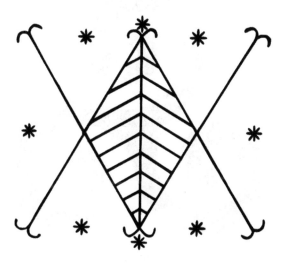

The Veves.
https://commons.wikimedia.org/wiki/File:VeveAyizan.svg

16. Yggdrasil

Yggdrasil.

17. The Triskele

The Triskele.

18. Mjolnir

Mjolnir.
https://commons.wikimedia.org/wiki/File:Mjollnir.png

19. Vegvisir

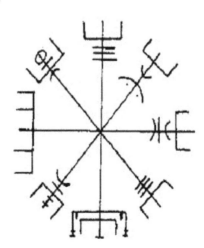

Vegvisir.
Jara Lisa, CC BY-SA 4.0 <https://creativecommons.org/licenses/by-sa/4.0>, via Wikimedia Commons https://commons.wikimedia.org/wiki/File:Vegvisir_de_Steven_Flowers.png

20. Valknut

Valknut.
https://commons.wikimedia.org/wiki/File:9crossings-knot-symmetric-triangles-quasi-valknut.svg

The Meaning of the Symbols

Now that you've had a chance to look at the symbols without a preconceived notion, you can delve into their purposes and applications. Here is a little background about them and their uses in their respective traditions.

1. The Celtic Knot

The Celtic knot is probably one of the most recognizable Pagan symbols. Typically presented as a series of knots forming a unique pattern, the symbol is often used in Celtic magic and Druidic practices. The Celtic knot can be found in religious manuscripts and architecture, representing the limitless power of the divine. In Celtic magic practices, it symbolizes the life cycle, birth, death, and rebirth, present in nature and human lives alike. You can incorporate it into different traditions designed to call on nature's infinite power, rejuvenation spells and rituals, fertility rites, and much more.

2. The Celtic Cross

After the Celtic Knot, the Celtic cross is the second most famous symbol utilized in traditional Pagan magic practices. It can also be found in architecture and monuments carved into stone. They can also be seen as independent stone monoliths made from wood or metal and shaped like a cross. In Celtic magic, the symbol has several interpretations. According to one, the four arms of the cross represent the four natural elements, water, fire, earth, and air. Another source showcases the symbol as the illustration of the four cardinal directions, east, west, north, and south. Apart from representing these, you can use the Celtic cross in your practices to represent the four seasons, the four stages of the day, or anything with four aspects.

3. The Triquetra

The triquetra is another Celtic pagan symbol used in Celtic magical traditions. It can be portrayed in several ways, usually in some form of three interlaced shapes, like Vesica Pisces or arcs. The symbol is often found in Celtic art, sometimes with a circle around it. The meaning of the three arcs varies depending on which interpretation you want to follow. For example, you can use it to represent and honor the Triple Goddess. It can also be employed to call on the power of the world's three realms of the world: sky, sea, and land.

4. The Five-Fold Symbol

The five-fold symbol also has Celtic pagan origins, but it's also often found in Scottish magic. According to ancient Scottish transitions, the symbol represents the different aspects contributing to the balance of human lives. In contemporary practices, it's often used to illustrate the four elements, fire, water, air, and earth, tied together by a fifth element, the universe itself. You can also use it to represent the four elements and the spirit or the five pillars of the universe, earth, air, sun, fire, and water.

5. The Spiral

Similarly to the previous one, the single spiral is also found in Scottish magic and was also a fundamental part of the ancient Celtic pagan culture. Physically illustrating a shape folded onto itself, the spiral represents infinite energy. Its waves are seen radiating outside, giving life to several different essences. According to one interpretation, the symbol showcases a person's life and the wisdom they've gathered from birth through life to death. You can also use it to gain awareness of your present and surroundings, to persevere against challenges, or to gather spiritual knowledge.

6. Ankh

Ankh is a crucial element in several African spiritual practices. It is believed to represent immortality and the divine mother, Isis. Nowadays, the symbol is used as the representation of life or the key to obtaining immortal life. It's incorporated into spiritual practices designed to elevate your level of consciousness, helping you reach a higher plane and become enlightened with infinite wisdom.

7. Winged Sun Disk

The winged sun disk symbol is also used in African spirituality as the representation of the sun god, or the sun itself, depending on the interpretation. If you're using it to honor the sun god, you're representing the creator of the universe. However, if you want to showcase the celestial body, you're celebrating life itself. Because without the sun, there wouldn't be life on earth. It can also be incorporated into practices for seeking spiritual elevation.

8. Adinkra

Adinkra is a symbol not unlike a simple drawing of a fern. It's used in African cultures. It's typically printed or painted on clothes, charms, and jewelry, often seen as a demonstration of spiritual power. Wearing this symbol will suggest to people that you're in control of your fate and will not let anyone else influence your life with their negative vibes. The symbol also means you have plans, love to work with people, and you'll do everything to obtain your goals.

9. The Serpent

The serpent is one of the most ancient symbols, and as such, it is used in different traditions. However, its most notable use is in Brujeria and Curanderismo, where it is integrated into transformative and healing spells and rituals. It's typically placed at the altar, in the middle of a protective circle, or onto any other sacred surface you use to perform your magical act. As a powerful being, the serpent will help you transform your life, go through a rebirth physically, mentally, and spiritually, and bring fertility into any area of your life.

10. The Helm of Awe

Also known as Aegishjalmur, the Helm of Awe is an ancient Norse symbol primarily used by Norse warriors who painted them on their forehead before going to a battle. Upon closer inspection, the symbol is seen as the combination of Isa and Algiz, two runes from the Elder Futhark. Isa symbolizes self-preservation, focus, and challenge. Whereas Algiz inspires victory and protection. In contemporary practices, this combined effect is used for empowerment when facing an illness, injury, or stressful situation. It can also help you ward off evil intentions, just as it worked to induce fear in the enemies of the Viking tribes. The symbol is shaped like a circle, which represents protection. The eight branches will ensure you can ward off evil intent no matter which direction it comes from. It'll help you overcome any challenge and become more aware of your own power.

11. The Hamsa

The word "hamsa" means "five" in Arabic, indicating the five fingers of a hand. The Hamsa is the symbol of protection in Jewish magic, and according to Kabbalah, it was used to invoke divine power, represented by the hand of God. Nowadays, it's still used for similar purposes, including in prayers and Kabbalistic rituals for different purposes. It is believed to protect against the Evil Eye (if that symbol is used for malicious intent) or evil in general. Use it within the scope of spells and rituals when you need an added layer of protection or when your energy is out of balance and you want to invite peace back into your life.

12. The Evil Eye

As mentioned above, envious people can use the Evil Eye to induce harm. However, it can also be helpful for warding off this type of energy. If you have anyone in your life that looks at your success and wonders what you have done to deserve this, their symbol will help you ward off their jealousy. It's recommended to wear it as a talisman whenever you interact with this person, and they'll soon cease their behavior. For added power, make sure you imbue the charm with the intention of keeping that person at bay. You can also combine it with other protective elements incorporated in Jewish folk magic traditions, such as wearing the charm on a red string bracelet.

13. The Tree of Life

While the tree of life is present in several traditions, in Jewish mysticism, it has a unique and powerful meaning. In Kabbalah, the Tree of Life is represented as a tree with ten branches, also referred to as the ten Sefirot. The ten Sefirot illustrate the different divine essence, the only form of God people can perceive and interact with. The symbol is used to invoke either one of these divine emanations through its rulers, the Archangels. Depending on which energy you need in your practice, you'll call on the Archangel that allows its distribution through the universe from their respective dominion.

---

14. Merkabah

A veve is a representation of an energetic force in African spiritual practices. These forces are spirits associated with elements of nature, its different powers, values, and emotions. The veves were initially made from flour or other powdery substance, which allowed people to invite the spirits' energy to one dedicated area. You can also draw or print veves on paper or any other surface and use them to attract a particular entity. Focusing on it will help you get them to reveal themselves in front of you.

15. The Veves

A veve is a representation of an energetic force in African spiritual practices. These are spirits associated with elements of nature, its different forces, values, and emotions. The veves are drawings, initially made from flour or other powdery substance, which allowed people to invite the spirits' energy to one dedicated area. You can also draw or print veves on paper or any other surface and use them to attract a particular entity. Focusing on it will help you get them to reveal themselves in front of you.

16. Yggdrasil

Yggdrasil, also called the Norse Tree of Life, is somewhat different from its Jewish counterpart. Not only does it have only nine branches (representing the nine realms of Norse mythology), but it has various tales and uses tied to it. According to one of these tales, Yggdrasil grew from the Well of Urd, the universal source of life. It's also believed that the Norse deities were eating their fruit to remain immortal. You can use Yggdrasil in rituals and spells where you want to make a connection to nature and the universe or reveal parts of your future. When used in meditation, it can also help you balance out your energies.

17. The Triskele

The Triskele, or the Horns of Odin, as it is called in Norse traditions, is a symbol with Celtic pagan origins. It's usually linked to Odin and his infinite power and wisdom. Hold it above your drink or meal and focus on infusing those with his power. When you consume some of it, you'll empower your own magic. It can also help you improve your communication skills and establish new connections in any area of your life.

18. Mjolnir

While most people are familiar with Mjolnir being the hammer of Thor, very few are aware of the magical significance of this tool. In ancient times, the Norse attributed lighting to Mjolnir being used against giants, their feared enemies. Therefore, Thor's hammer has become a symbol of protection, as it's used in modern Norse magical practices too. When incorporated into protection rituals and spells you perform before you begin to work, it can safeguard you from malicious intent during magical work. Wear it as a talisman, a charm, or a necklace, and it will also protect you in your day-to-day life.

19. Vegvisir

Vegvisir is a Norse symbol with eight branches held up by a central pillar. There are several interpretations of what the branches mean. According to one, they represent the expanded directions, south, southwest, southeast, north, northwest, northeast, west, and east. Another lore says the branches represent eight out of the nine worlds of Norse mythology, with the center being the ninth world. In modern times, practitioners use this symbol for guidance when they aren't sure if they're headed in the right direction or have lost their way completely. You can also wear it as a talisman, and it'll protect you just as it did the Viking ships during vicious storms. It can also guide you through challenging situations or when you feel you've lost part of yourself due to emotional trauma. It will boost your confidence in your ability to persevere against the odds, allowing you to achieve this goal. Another way to incorporate the symbol into your practice is to enhance it with magic and give it to someone as a good luck charm to attract love and prosperity.

20. Valknut

Valknut, or Odin's knot, as it's called in Norse mythology, is the ultimate symbol of death. It was used to honor the fallen warriors and help them cross onto Valhalla, Hel, and other afterlife realms. According to another interpretation, Valknut can provide protection for the souls who passed on. Wearing it as a talisman, you can also use it to draw Odin's power to help you with spiritual communication. It will shield you and the friendly spirit you are trying to contact through the realms from malicious spirits.

Infusing the Symbols with Magic

Once you've found the symbol or symbols you wish to use in your craft, you must prepare them and yourself for their use. The first step in this process is cleansing your mind and body. This will ensure that your power remains pure, and you won't have any negative vibes affecting the symbols' magic. You can do this by taking a cleaning bath, performing breathing exercises, smudging your body, or through any other purification ritual of your choice. Smudging can also be used to eradicate any negative influence from the room or space you'll use or set up your magical tools. Smudging is a simple process that involves lighting a small bunch of dried herbs on fire and letting their smoke permeate and cleanse every corner of your space. When doing this, move around to ensure no negative energy remains, and pass over the symbols several times.

Once you've ascertained that the symbols are ready to be infused with positive energy, you can focus on this task. Be as clear and concise as possible when forming an intention. This will make the process smoother. For example, if you want a character to serve as protection, you'll need to express this. You'll need to say that you need the symbol to carry protective magic. If you require healing, a good luck charm, attracting love, or financial prosperity, then you ask for those. Depending on your purpose and experience, you may need more time to infuse the symbols with the desired form of magic. There are several ways to go about when doing this, and the choice will often depend on your intention and personal preferences. Here are some techniques to imbue symbols with magic:

- **Meditation:** This approach takes only a few minutes a day and allows you to submerge into your thoughts while keeping the symbol or charm in your hands. Take a deep breath and focus on sending your energy toward the sign. It also helps awaken the character's own magic. You can either close your eyes and visualize the symbols in front of you or keep them open and look at the symbol until it's ready to use.

- **Journeying:** Similarly to meditation, journeying also requires a deep focus, which will help focus your thoughts on the symbol and your intention. During your journey, you may also ask a spiritual guide to help you empower the sign you are holding in your hands.

- **Prayers and offerings:** If you're working with a higher spiritual being, or your symbol is associated with them, you can ask them to give you the ability to infuse the magical tool with your intent, magic, and perhaps their magic too. Prayers and offerings are great ways to express gratitude for whatever help you get from the symbols.

- **Dreams:** Keeping symbols near your body while sleeping is an ancient tradition that involves the activation of magical tools. You can draw or print symbols on paper and place them under your pillow. Or, you can put the tool or charm on your nightstand, look at them before going to sleep, repeat your intention in your head, and go to bed.

- **Using celestial bodies:** Many cultures use the power of the sun and the moon to enrich and activate magical tools. This is usually combined with other intention-boosting and charm-activating techniques. For example, you can place the symbols under the moonlight at the full moon and meditate on your intention by sitting nearby and gazing at the moon.

- **Using the elements:** The natural and celestial elements can also be used to infuse magical tools like symbols with positive intentions and magic. For this, you'll need an altar or any other sacred space where you can place the sign and the representations of the elements around it. Ask the elements to help consecrate the symbols and allow you to channel your intention toward them.

- **Wearing them:** Some symbols will benefit from staying close to your body. This will ensure your intention is engraved into them. It also works for infusing personal magic. There are symbols you can keep wearing on or near your body even after they've been infused with magic, especially if the spell or ritual they are used in requires this. You can also draw a symbol on a piece of paper and put it in your pocket or bag for the required duration.

How long it takes to prepare your symbols depends on several factors. It may take more time to ensure they are ready to use before you delve into any magical practice. Check this by feeling their energy. If it's aligned with yours and you can feel their magic, you're good to go. If not, you'll need to put more effort into infusing the symbols. You'll need to truly want it to lead you to your goals, so keep your focus on the task and trust your intuition. It will show you the way, as no other guide will ever be able to.

Chapter 10: Your Folk Magic Spellbook

Rituals and spellwork can seem complicated at the beginning, and feeling lost during this time is completely normal for someone just starting on this journey. Spellwork is broadly defined as the technique of using certain words and gestures in combination with herbs, candles, or other charms and symbols. Spellwork has always been an important part of folk magic cultures and religions. It is the foundation of folk magic, helping draw energy from a different plane of existence. This energy is then imbued into this world by using sacred words, gestures, and other practices.

Spellwork has always been an important part of folk magic cultures and religions.
https://www.pexels.com/photo/a-spell-book-and-gem-stone-on-the-window-seal-6806397/

Spellwork is a lot like physical exercise. As consistency and practice help strengthen your muscles, the same goes for spellwork. When you repeat and practice a spell consistently, you'll ultimately be able to manifest your desires. As you continue practicing various spells, you'll find yourself working alongside your intuition and, soon enough, mastering the art of spellwork. Often, you may not get the results you desire from rituals and spellwork, but don't let this discourage you. Just because a spell works for one person does not mean it will work for another.

The accuracy and flow of your spellwork will improve with time and practice, but you have to start somewhere. This chapter will act as a beginner's guide to spellwork and rituals as practiced in various folk magic cultures.

Wiccan Celtic Magic

To Honor a Deceased Loved One

Intent: To honor a deceased loved one and deal with your grief. This ritual will help you cope with the loss you've experienced.

Things You'll Need

- A picture of your deceased loved one. Make sure it is a spare photo or a copy you won't miss
- Some memorabilia of your loved one, such as a necklace, ring, or some other piece associated with them
- Your preferred drink, coffee, tea, or anything else
- A thin, medium-sized, white candle
- A lighter or matches
- A marker or pen

Method

1. Choose a day for the ritual. It should be a day you associate with your loved one, like their death anniversary or their birthday.
2. Sit in a comfortable place along with the supplies you've gathered for this ritual.
3. Light the candle, pour your favorite beverage, and relax in the moment. Erase all thoughts from your mind. Only think of the person you've lost and let yourself feel the grief.

4. Take a sip from your drink, and start writing a personal letter to your deceased loved one on the back of their picture. Write down everything you wanted to say to them, and bid them farewell.

5. At the end of the letter, write: "The meaning of this spell will be gone but never forgotten."

6. After you're done with the letter, read it aloud to get it across to the spirit of your loved one.

7. Finish your drink while letting the candle burn out, then fold the picture as many times as you can.

8. Keep this picture safe, and when you visit the grave of your loved one, bury it near their gravestone along with the memorabilia.

Purification Spell

Intent: to eliminate a negative feeling, entity, situation, or person from your life.

What You'll Need

- Sea salt
- A lighter or matches
- Cumin
- A black colored ribbon
- A pen and paper
- A glass jar
- A small dish
- An offering or item associated with the person or situation you're trying to remove

Method

1. Take a small jar and place some cumin inside it until it's half full.

2. Then, take a spoonful of sea salt and place it on top of the cumin.

3. Take a piece of paper and write down the name, feeling, or situation that is troubling you. Put this paper in a non-flammable dish and light it.

4. Once the paper has burned completely, take the ashes from the dish and place them on top of the sea salt inside the glass jar.

5. Fasten the lid of the jar as tightly as you can, and every night before bed, shake this jar as many times as you want. While you do this, picture the situation or person slowly moving away from your life. Repeat this until the next full moon.

6. Once the full moon arrives, tie the black ribbon around the glass jar and go to a river, beach, or lake.

7. Either throw or place the glass jar into the water along with the offering you've selected and watch it drift away. Walk away from this place without looking back.

Recovery Spell

Intent: To help yourself recover from whatever troubles you've faced and gain your sense of self-worth back. This spell is ideal for healing from a traumatic event.

What You'll Need

- Thyme
- Mint
- Sea salt or pink Himalayan salt
- Rose quartz
- A lily
- A rose
- Some bay leaves
- Olive oil
- Cinnamon
- A small sealable jug or bottle
- A cooking pot
- Some water

Method

1. Fill the cooking pot with water and put it on the stove to heat.

2. Once the water has boiled, add the flower petals from the rose and lily flowers. Next, add a pinch of Himalayan salt and some oil into the boiling water. Keep mixing as you add the ingredients.

3. Finally, add the thyme, mint, and cinnamon into the pot and stir slowly. While you're stirring, say the words:

4. "I forgive myself and love myself despite everything that's happened to me. I accept the suffering and let it move forward with me. My past doesn't define me, and neither does my pain or misfortune. I accept myself as I am and let my inner light shine through."

5. Repeat this spell three times while slowly stirring the potion, and pour it into the jar when it's done.

6. Later that day, take this potion and add it to your shower or bath routine while holding the rose quartz crystal. This will ensure that all your negative energy is sucked out and your energy is replenished.

7. Keep this bottle with you, and use it whenever you need to recover or heal from something.

African Spirituality

Gris Gris

Intent: Gris Gris bags are used to bring you prosperity and fortune. These mojo bags are considered the most powerful piece of charm in Voodoo magic. They assist in all matters of life with the right intent by empowering their owners. Many consider it a prayer in a bag.

What You'll Need

- A piece of fabric
- A string or elastic band
- Some sacred herbs of your choice (basil, lavender, dandelion, ivy, marigold, or any other herbs mentioned in the previous chapters)
- A few crystals (Quartz, tourmaline, emerald, selenite, malachite, or any other crystals of your choice)
- Shells or unique stones
- Talismans or charms of your choice
- A small candle

Method

1. Gather all the materials and sit in a comfortable space to make your Gris Gris bag.

2. Light the candle first, and lay out the piece of fabric on the floor or on a table.

3. Place each item you've selected on top of the fabric, one at a time.

4. When placing each item onto the fabric, set your intention onto that charm and then place it inside. For instance, you can set the intent for attracting love, prosperity, success, or anything that you desire.

5. Bring all four corners of the fabric together at the top so that the fabric forms a small bag, and tie it up using a long string.

Crossroads Magic

Intent: Crossroads magic is one of the most powerful sources of sacred practice in Hoodoo and Voodoo magic cultures. Crossroads are where two roads intersect. According to folklore, the crossroads of conjure is where the real world and the spirit world connect. Therefore, crossroads of any kind hold a special value in ancient magic practices. One such spell ensures that all blockages from your path are eliminated.

What You'll Need

- Twenty-one coins or pennies
- Three red candles
- Lighter or matches

Method

1. Find a crossroad that you think best portrays the current situation of your life that's troubling you.

2. Stand in the middle of the crossroad and set the intent of the ritual. Visualize the difficulties you're facing, and count all the obstacles in your path.

3. Place the coins at the crossroad along with the three red candles.

4. Light the candles and wait for them to burn out while you chant some spells.

5. As the candles burn out, visualize all the obstacles and troubles being erased from your path or your "crossroads."

Brujeria and Curanderismo

Los Siete Nudos (The Seven Knots)

Intent: Perform this unique ritual to eliminate seven problems in your life. It will help either solve or eliminate these issues.

What You'll Need

- A red ribbon (2 ft)
- A candle
- A small jar

Method

1. Sit in a comfortable position where you won't be disturbed for the entirety of the ritual.

2. Take the ribbon in your hands, and visualize seven problems that need to be solved in your life.

3. Think of each problem individually, and while doing so, tie a knot in the ribbon.

4. The first knot should be right in the middle of the complete length of the ribbon.

5. The second and third knots should be about four inches to the left and right of the first knot, respectively.

6. The fourth and fifth knots should be four inches away from the second and third knots.

7. The sixth knot should be on the left side of the ribbon, towards the end. Lastly, the seventh knot should connect one end of the ribbon to the other end, binding the problems that trouble you.

8. Place this ribbon into the jar and seal it. Bury the jar far away from where you live to make sure it doesn't get dug up. Also, ensure that you do this ritual alone, or else the spell won't be as effective.

Agua Bendita (Holy Water)

Intent: As an all-purpose, healing, recovery, and protection product, holy water is the best way to cleanse your soul. The quality of holy water depends on how the ritual is carried out.

What You'll Need

- A stick of palo santo (holy wood)
- A silver bullion
- A copper container

Method

1. Place the copper container where there's rainwater in order to collect enough to prepare the holy water. Make sure you collect clear, pure rainwater and not drain water.

2. Place the silver bullion and palo santo stick in the water, and allow them to permeate the water.

3. Once you feel the water has been infused properly, expose it to direct sunlight, where it will gather the energy of light.

4. Finally, pour the holy water into a glass bottle and use it to anoint or asperge the patient during treatment.

Norse Spellwork

Healing Magic

Intent: To heal any sufferings, diseases, or ailments incurred. This spell will help cure any illness or injury.

What You'll Need

- The sacred cauldron
- Mountain ash berries
- Vervain
- Feverfew
- Candles and matches
- A parchment and pencil

Method

1. This ritual is best performed during the waning moon phase. Start by placing the offerings on a platter, and light the candle. These should include the above-mentioned herbs or any alternative herbs.

2. On the piece of parchment, draw a rough sketch of the sick or injured person. This drawing does not need to be perfect; even

the sketch of a stick figure will do. Don't forget to write their name at the bottom of the parchment.

3. Now, tap the cauldron with a wand, and chant the following spell:

4. "Oh great cauldron of rebirth and renewal, hear my call and heal (name) of all sickness. Rebuild their body, spirit, and mind."

5. Next, tap the piece of parchment with your wand three times and set it aflame using the candle. Drop this parchment into the cauldron and let it burn. While it's burning, chant this:

6. "All illness turns to ashes; all that was wrong is now right; my words have reached Asgard; your healing will come tonight."

7. Once the parchment turns to ashes, add the herb offerings into the cauldron and let it cool.

8. Finally, take the ashes and herbs and bury them in the ground to eliminate the illness.

Love Spell

Intent: To bring you the love you desire, whether romantic or otherwise. This love spell is incredibly potent and effective.

What You'll Need

- The sacred cauldron
- A pink candle
- A candle holder
- A red rose
- A vase
- Rose blossom oil
- A small bell

Method

1. The altar for this spell should be set up two days in advance before the full moon. Place the pink candle inside the candle holder and put it in the cauldron. The red rose will go into the vase, which will be kept beside the cauldron.

2. On the night of the full moon, start the ritual by grabbing the handle with both hands and pouring feelings of love into it. Do not light the candle before the full moon appears.

3. Use a knife or dagger to carve a rune of true love on the candle and place the candle inside the cauldron. Finally, light the candle, and ring the bell three times. Chant:

4. "As the flame of this candle grows brighter, Freyre, lord of love, please bring me love's ever-burning fire. Then, as the flame flickers low, Freyre, do give to me a true love, heart to heart."

5. Ring the bell three more times, and stay at the altar until the candle has completely burned out.

Spellwork is indeed a delicate part of magic and should be done with the utmost care and focus. While it does take a while to practice, once you're familiar with the processes, you'll start to see real outcomes from your practice. However, make sure you don't rush the process of learning spellwork, rituals, and herb magic. This is something that requires time, patience, and, most importantly, skill.

Conclusion

Folk magic has been a part of human culture since early civilizations, but it was deemed an acceptable practice only recently. While many people often associate magic with Wiccan or Pagan cultures, its scope is, in reality, much greater. It includes Norse paganism, African spirituality, Jewish magic, and countless other magic-practicing cultures. Hopefully, reading this book will have provided you with a clearer picture of what folk magic is and how it lives on. For many people, learning about these practices is often life-changing. This is because it finally allows them to know which culture they most connect with and get to start their journey along this path.

Once you select which folk magic practice to follow, you'll go through tremendous personal changes as your entire belief system matures and evolves. Moreover, you'll find a community full of supportive and encouraging people who'll help you along your journey. At times, the multitude of ideas and concepts may overwhelm you, so make sure you don't lose your way. To master any subject, you must understand the fundamental concepts, and magic practices are no exception. Once you've learned the basics of a specific folk magic culture, nothing can stop you from becoming an expert.

We suggest you go through the last three chapters in detail to avoid any mistakes while practicing, especially if it's your first attempt. The sacred plants and herbs in any culture are sacred for a reason, as they provide numerous benefits and play a special role in magic rituals. Learning about these herbs will be the first step to mastering the art of spells and rituals. Once you've learned the signs, symbols, and charms associated with each culture, you'll be in a much better position to understand more complex spells and rituals. Also, make sure to follow the spells provided in the last chapter as precisely as you can. Altering even the smallest step can end up making the spell impotent or completely useless.

Once you've grasped a broad understanding of these folk magic cultures, you can move on to learning about the one or ones you're most interested in. By now, you know their history and basics, but there's still a lot to learn. So, as you start on this journey of great spiritual learning, don't hold yourself back from getting all the information required. Most of all, start practicing the traditions that speak to you, which will bring you one step closer to discovering your true self.

Lastly, but importantly, remember that those who practice magic (of any kind) often form close-knit communities. If you ever feel you cannot grasp a particular concept, or perform a specific ritual or spell, don't hesitate to reach out to those who you think may offer assistance. In the meantime, keep this book by your side whenever you need to revisit the fundamentals of folk magic. Good luck!

Here's another book by Mari Silva that you might like

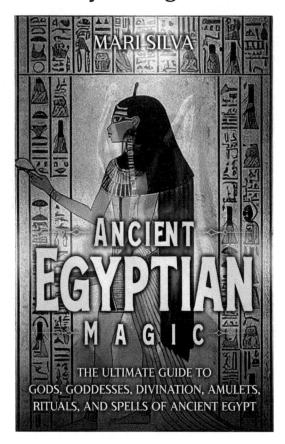

Your Free Gift
(only available for a limited time)

Thanks for getting this book! If you want to learn more about various spirituality topics, then join Mari Silva's community and get a free guided meditation MP3 for awakening your third eye. This guided meditation mp3 is designed to open and strengthen ones third eye so you can experience a higher state of consciousness. Simply visit the link below the image to get started.

https://spiritualityspot.com/meditation

References

Beyer, C. (2012, August 11). Folk Magic. Learn Religions. https://www.learnreligions.com/folk-magic-95826

Claire, H. (2018, July 2). How to use folk magic. Llewellyn Worldwide. https://www.llewellyn.com/journal/article/2701

Coles, D. (2020, October 21). An introduction to hoodoo. Cosmopolitan. https://www.cosmopolitan.com/lifestyle/a34115081/hoodoo-vs-voodoo-facts-history/

Savage, W. (2017, November 29). "Cunning Folk": Witchcraft, healing, and superstition. Pen and Pension. https://penandpension.com/2017/11/29/cunning-folk-witchcraft-healing-and-superstition/

Scott. (2016, May 28). Folk magic, witchcraft, whats the difference? Cailleach's Herbarium. https://cailleachs-herbarium.com/2016/05/folk-magic-witchcraft-whats-the-difference/

Shippey, A. (2018, January 19). Who were the cunning folk? — Lord♀Matria. Lord♀Matria. https://austinshippey.com/blog/2018/1/19/who-were-the-cunning-folk

Waldron, D. (2014). Folk Magic. In Encyclopedia of Psychology and Religion (pp. 675–676). Springer US.

Wigington, P. (2019, December 28). Folk magic Powwow: History and practices. Learn Religions. https://www.learnreligions.com/Powwow-folk-magic-4779937

Adebare, O. (2022, April 28). Celebrating Black history & Black culture. I AM History. https://www.iamhistory.co.uk/home/10-african-gods-to-know

After life beliefts in voodoo Religion. (n.d.). Haiti Observer. http://www.haitiobserver.com/blog/after-life-beliefts-in-voodoo-religion.html

Alvarez, L. (1997, January 27). After years of secrecy, Santeria is suddenly much more popular. And public. The New York Times. https://www.nytimes.com/1997/01/27/nyregion/after-years-of-secrecy-santeria-is-suddenly-much-more-popular-and-public.html

Beyer, C. (2010, February 1). An introduction to the basic beliefs of the vodou (Voodoo) religion. Learn Religions. https://www.learnreligions.com/vodou-an-introduction-for-beginners-95712

Cuthbert, M. (2021, September 23). Kemetism religion. World Religions. https://world-religions.info/kemetism-religion/

Gleimius, N. (2022, September 2). African gods: Deities, belief systems, and legends of Africa. TheCollector. https://www.thecollector.com/african-gods-legends-of-africa-gods/

Kemetic Society. (n.d.). Educationforlifeacademy.com. https://educationforlifeacademy.com/kemetic-society

Traditional African ways of worshiping god. (n.d.). ATIKA SCHOOL. https://www.atikaschool.org/kcsecrenotes/traditional-african-ways-of-worshiping-god

Wigington, P. (2011, November 15). What is the Santeria religion? Learn Religions. https://www.learnreligions.com/about-santeria-traditions-2562543

Alcamo, B. (2021, October 20). Brujería: Getting witchy in Latin America. JP Linguistics - French, Italian, Spanish Classes in NYC. https://www.jplinguistics.com/spanish-blog/brujera-getting-witchy-in-latin-america

Benner, M. (2018, July 17). Curanderismo, the Traditional Healing of Mexican Culture. Four Directions Wellness. https://fourdirectionswellness.com/2018/07/17/curanderismo-the-traditional-healing-of-mexican-culture/

Cultural terms. (n.d.). Curanderismo. https://www.curanderismo.org/culturalterms

Gomez, S. (2020, July 31). Santería & brujería: Two religious practices embedded in the Latin American and Afro-Caribbean cultures. BELatina.

Martinez, J. (2020, September 25). Why more Afro-Latinas are embracing African spiritual and wellness practices. Oprah Daily. https://www.oprahdaily.com/life/a34130848/afro-latina-african-spiritual-wellness-bruja-trend/

Padilla, R., Gomez, V., Biggerstaff, S. L., & Mehler, P. S. (2001). Use of curanderismo in a public health care system. Archives of Internal Medicine, 161(10), 1336–1340. https://doi.org/10.1001/archinte.161.10.1336

Ruelas, V. (2020, December 21). How brujería helped me heal. Cosmopolitan. https://www.cosmopolitan.com/lifestyle/a34979780/brujeria-explained-by-brujas/

Salazar, C. L., & Levin, J. (2013). Religious features of curanderismo training and practice. Explore (New York, N.Y.), 9(3), 150–158. https://doi.org/10.1016/j.explore.2013.02.003

Snider, A. C. (2019, October 11). Bruja meaning explained. Teen Vogue. https://www.teenvogue.com/story/brujeria-meaning-explained

Torres, N., Froeschle, J., Torres, H., & Hicks, J. (n.d.). Cultural Awareness: Understanding Curanderismo. Counseling.org. https://www.counseling.org/docs/default-source/vistas/article_396cfd25f16116603abcacff0000bee5e7.pdf?sfvrsn=f2eb45 2c_4

Trotter, R. T., Chavira, J. A., & Robert T. Trotter II (Arizona Regents' Professor, Department of Anthropology, Northern Arizona University, Flagstaff, USA). (1997). Curanderismo: Mexican American folk healing (2nd ed.). University of Georgia Press.

Ulloa, G. (2021, October 11). The ancient practice of curanderismo is getting A modern makeover. The Zoe Report. https://www.thezoereport.com/wellness/curanderismo-healing-practice-ritual

Wigington, P. (2012, March 28). What is a bruja or brujo in witchcraft? Learn Religions. https://www.learnreligions.com/what-is-a-bruja-or-brujo-2561875

Wigington, P. (2015, October 24). Curanderismo: The folk magic of Mexico. Learn Religions. https://www.learnreligions.com/curanderismo-the-folk-magic-of-mexico-2562500

Woodman, S. (2018, March 13). What to know about the origins of Mexican folk healing. Culture Trip; The Culture Trip. https://theculturetrip.com/north-america/mexico/articles/everything-to-know-about-mexican-folk-healing/

Allen Cross, J. (2022, April 19). 3 Limpias to turn your luck around. Spirituality & Health. https://www.spiritualityhealth.com/3-limpias-to-turn-your-luck-around

Swerdloff, A. (2016, October 28). How to do an egg cleanse for your aura. VICE. https://www.vice.com/en/article/wnbxnn/cleanse-your-aura-with-the-power-of-eggs

Athame, & Stang. (2017, December 26). Nicnevin: The Scottish witch mother. By Athame and Stang. https://www.patheos.com/blogs/byathameandstang/2017/12/nicnevin-scottish-witch-mother/

Campsie, A. (2019, October 17). 9 charms, spells and cures used by Highland witches. The Scotsman. https://www.scotsman.com/heritage-and-retro/heritage/9-charms-spells-and-cures-used-highland-witches-1404985

Fee. (2021, January 18). Older than time: The myth of the Cailleach, the great mother. Wee White Hoose; Fee. https://weewhitehoose.co.uk/study/the-cailleach/

hag o the hills. (2015, December 17). Traditional Scottish divination. Hag o' The Hills. https://hagothehills.wordpress.com/2015/12/17/traditional-scottish-divination/

Living Liminally. (n.d.). Blogspot.com.

Lou Chaika, B. (2020, October 16). The Cailleach: A witch for our times. EarthSanctuaries; Betty Lou Chaika. https://earthsanctuaries.net/the-cailleach-a-witch-for-our-times/

Scott. (2015, September 7). What is Scottish Witchcraft (or not)? - the role of the wise women. Cailleach's Herbarium. https://cailleachs-herbarium.com/2015/09/what-is-scottish-witchcraft-or-not-the-role-of-the-wise-women/

Scott. (2017, April 24). Who the hell is Sidhe? – Fairy Faith and Animism in Scotland. A Challenge to Divinity. Cailleach's Herbarium. https://cailleachs-herbarium.com/2017/04/who-the-hell-is-sidhe-fairy-faith-and-animism-in-scotland-a-challenge-to-divinity/

Scott. (2019, February 10). Saining not smudging- purification and lustration in Scottish folk magic practice. Cailleach's Herbarium. https://cailleachs-herbarium.com/2019/02/saining-not-smudging-purification-and-lustration-in-scottish-folk-magic-practice/

Smith, K. (2019, August 16). Which witch is which? A history of Scottish witchcraft. Scottish Field. https://www.scottishfield.co.uk/culture/which-witch-is-which-a-history-of-scottish-witchcraft/

Surhone, L. M., Tennoe, M. T., & Henssonow, S. F. (Eds.). (2010). National library of Scotland. Betascript Publishing.

The origin and lore of Fairies and fairy land. (2015, August 14). Eric Edwards Collected Works. https://ericwedwards.wordpress.com/2015/08/14/the-origin-and-lore-of-fairies-and-fairy-land/

Wright, G. (2020a, August 16). Cailleach. Mythopedia. https://mythopedia.com/topics/cailleach

Wright, G. (2020b, August 16). Lugh. Mythopedia. https://mythopedia.com/topics/lugh

Blakemore, E. (2019, November 15). Druids—facts and information. National Geographic. https://www.nationalgeographic.com/history/article/why-know-little-druids

Info. (2019, April 25). Druid. Order of Bards, Ovates & Druids; OBOD. https://druidry.org/

Meitner, L., & Johnson, J. H. (2016, November 14). Humanist common ground: Paganism. American Humanist Association. https://americanhumanist.org/paths/paganism/

The Religion of the Ancient Celts: Chapter XXI. Magic. (n.d.). Sacred-texts.com. https://www.sacred-texts.com/neu/celt/rac/rac24.htm

Who were the Druids? (2017, March 21). Historic UK. https://www.historic-uk.com/HistoryUK/HistoryofWales/Druids/

BBC News. (2015, February 14). Iceland's Asatru pagans reach new height with first temple. BBC. https://www.bbc.com/news/world-europe-31437973

Cragle, J. M. (2017). Contemporary Germanic/Norse paganism and recent survey data. Pomegranate The International Journal of Pagan Studies, 19(1), 77–116.

Dan. (2012, November 14). Norse mythology for Smart People - the ultimate online guide to Norse mythology and religion. Norse Mythology for Smart People. https://norse-mythology.org/

Norse mythology. (2016, October 27). English History. https://englishhistory.net/vikings/norse-mythology/

Routes North. (2022, June 20). Norse Paganism: what is it, and what do its followers believe? Routes North. https://www.routesnorth.com/language-and-culture/norse-paganism/

Wiles, K. (n.d.). Who are the vikings? Historytoday.com. https://www.historytoday.com/who-are-vikings

אמור, א. (2020) .אמור, א. (2020, October 21). The Tree of Life and the 10 Sefirot. Derehateva.Co.Il. https://www.derehateva.co.il/2020/10/21/the-tree-of-life-and-the-10-sefirot/?lang=en

Sefirot - Tree of Life. (n.d.). Geneseo.Edu. https://www.geneseo.edu/yoga/sefirot-tree-life

My Jewish Learning. (2003, February 10). Kabbalah and Mysticism 101. My Jewish Learning. https://www.myjewishlearning.com/article/kabbalah-mysticism-101/

Immanuel Schochet, J. (2003, September 22). Jewish Mysticism: Why Is It Unique? Chabad.Org. https://www.chabad.org/library/article_cdo/aid/380317/jewish/Jewish-Mysticism-Why-Is-It-Unique.htm

Kabbalah and Jewish Mysticism. (n.d.). Jewfaq.Org. https://www.jewfaq.org/kabbalah.htm

My Jewish Learning. (2006, October 29). Do Jews Believe In Angels? My Jewish Learning. https://www.myjewishlearning.com/article/angels/

My Jewish Learning. (2008, October 23). Jewish Magical Practices and Beliefs. My Jewish Learning. https://www.myjewishlearning.com/article/jewish-magical-practices-beliefs/

Angels & Angelology. (n.d.). Jewishvirtuallibrary.Org. https://www.jewishvirtuallibrary.org/angels-and-angelology-2

Hopler, W. (n.d.). Who Are the Angels on the Kabbalah Tree of Life? Learn Religions https://www.learnreligions.com/angels-kabbalah-tree-of-life-124294

11 spiritual meaning of cinnamon: What this spice means for your life. (2022, August 17). Naturalscents.net. https://naturalscents.net/spirituality/spiritual-meaning-of-cinnamon-170

A sage smudging ritual to cleanse your aura & clear your space. (2015, March 13). Mindbodygreen. https://www.mindbodygreen.com/articles/smudging-101-burning-sage

Aboriginal sacred plants: Sage. (2013, March 18). Ictinc.Ca. https://www.ictinc.ca/blog/aboriginal-sacred-plants-sage

About. (n.d.). Doebay.com http://doebay.com/wp-content/pages/spices_and_herbs_that_spell_casters_can_use_on_spells_to_bring_love.html

Ancestral herbalism and Samhain: Working deeply with Rosemary. (2019, October 27). The Druids Garden. https://thedruidsgarden.com/2019/10/27/ancestral-herbalism-and-samhain-working-deeply-with-rosemary/

Avia. (2018, March 30). Symbolic mistletoe meaning: More than just Christmas decorations! Whats-your-sign.com; Whats-Your-Sign. https://www.whats-your-sign.com/symbolic-mistletoe-meaning-more-than-christmas-decorations.html

Cervantes-Curandera, P. (2016, October 27). What is the Day of the Dead. Institute of Shamanism and Curanderismo. https://www.instituteofshamanismandcuranderismo.com/what-is-the-day-of-the-dead/

Chamomile magical properties. (n.d.). AromaG's Botanica. https://www.aromagregory.com/product/chamomile/

Cinnamon: Spiritual meaning, uses & benefits. (n.d.). Enter The Stargate https://www.enterthestargate.com/blogs/plant-profiles/cinnamon

Dictionary.com. (2020, December 23). What is "mistletoe" and why do we kiss under it? Dictionary.com. https://www.dictionary.com/e/mistletoe/

Ellis, E. (2021, October 29). Oak Spring Garden foundation - the world's most magical plants. Oak Spring Garden Foundation. https://www.osgf.org/blog/2021/10/25/the-most-magical-plants

Greenwood, C. (2021, September 15). 10 spiritual benefits of cinnamon (love, manifestation, protection, cleansing and more). Outofstress.com. https://www.outofstress.com/cinnamon-spiritual-benefits/

Greenwood, C. (2022a, February 3). 10 spiritual benefits of chamomile (+ how to use it for protection & prosperity). Outofstress.com. https://www.outofstress.com/chamomile-spiritual-benefits/

Greenwood, C. (2022b, May 18). 9 spiritual benefits of mugwort (feminine energy, sleep magic, cleansing and more). Outofstress.com. https://www.outofstress.com/spiritual-benefits-mugwort/

Herb magic catalogue: Rosemary leaves. (n.d.). Herbmagic.com. https://www.herbmagic.com/rosemary.html

Herbs for visionary work at the winter solstice. (2020, December 20). The Druids Garden. https://thedruidsgarden.com/2020/12/20/herbs-for-visionary-work-at-the-winter-solstice/

Jinn, P. (2022, May 25). Frankincense: 5000 years of scent and spirituality. Pink Jinn. https://www.pinkjinn.com/2022/05/25/frankincense-5000-years-of-scent-and-spirituality/

Lets get ritualistic: Frankincense. (n.d.). In Fiore. https://infiore.net/blogs/journal/ingredient-spotlight-frankincense

Magickal properties of mugwort. (n.d.). Grove and Grotto https://www.groveandgrotto.com/blogs/articles/magickal-properties-of-mugwort

Martinelli, S. (2020, May 23). Botanical magic: Plants in Myth and folklore. Three Leaf Farm. https://www.threeleaffarm.com/blog/botanical-magic-plants-in-myth-and-folklore

Merry berry: magical mistletoe. (n.d.). National Trust. https://www.nationaltrust.org.uk/features/merry-berry-magical-mistletoe

Michelle, H. (2018, December 21). Mistletoe magick for healing, fertility and protection. Witch on Fire. https://www.patheos.com/blogs/witchonfire/2018/12/mistletoe-magick-for-love-and-protection/

Moodymoons, P. by. (2015, December 3). 10 magickal uses for cinnamon. Moody Moons. https://www.moodymoons.com/2015/12/03/10-magickal-uses-for-cinnamon/

Moodymoons, P. by. (2016, March 7). 10 magickal uses for sage. Moody Moons. https://www.moodymoons.com/2016/03/07/10-magickal-uses-for-sage/

Moodymoons, P. by. (2022, April 4). Using mugwort in witchcraft & spells. Moody Moons. https://www.moodymoons.com/2022/04/04/using-mugwort-in-witchcraft-spells/

Moone, A. (2019, May 28). Magical properties of cinnamon. Plentiful Earth. https://plentifulearth.com/magical-properties-of-cinnamon-cinnamon-materia-magicka/

Morningbird. (2019a, November 1). Chamomile. The Witchipedia. https://witchipedia.com/book-of-shadows/herblore/chamomile/

Morningbird. (2019b, November 1). Cinnamon. The Witchipedia. https://witchipedia.com/book-of-shadows/herblore/cinnamon/

Northern tradition shamanism: The nine sacred herbs. (n.d.). Northernshamanism.org. http://www.northernshamanism.org/the-nine-sacred-herbs.html

Organic African sage smudge stick - Etsy UK. (n.d.). Etsy.com. https://www.etsy.com/listing/835313545/organic-african-sage-smudge-stick

Plants and herbs used for magic. (n.d.). Bluerelicsflowers.com. https://www.bluerelicsflowers.com/Plants-and-Herbs-Used-for-Magic

Published by J. (2020, February 19). Chamomile folklore and magical uses. Marble Crow. https://marblecrowblog.com/2020/02/19/chamomile-folklore-and-magical-uses/

Rhys, D. (2020, August 12). What is the symbolism of mistletoe? Symbol Sage. https://symbolsage.com/mistletoe-meaning-and-symbolism/

Rhys, D. (2021, June 21). Sage herb - meaning and symbolism. Symbol Sage. https://symbolsage.com/sage-herb-meaning-symbolism/

Ritual tools: Sacred work with Mugwort. (n.d.). Circle Sanctuary. https://www.circlesanctuary.org/index.php/circle-magazine/sample-articles/ritual-tools-sacred-work-with-mugwort

Shade, P. (n.d.). The supernatural side of plants – CornellBotanicGardens. Cornellbotanicgardens.org. https://cornellbotanicgardens.org/the-supernatural-side-of-plants/

Silva, J. (2021, October 26). 11 Rosemary magical properties and spiritual uses. Angelical Balance. https://www.angelicalbalance.com/spiritual-protection/rosemary-magical-properties/

Silva, J. (2022, July 22). 9 spiritual meanings and benefits of frankincense. Angelical Balance. https://www.angelicalbalance.com/spirituality/spiritual-meaning-benefits-of-frankincense/

Stuff, C. V. P. (2022, October 5). Rosemary spiritual meaning: How to utilize this powerful herb. Coachella Valley Preserve. https://coachellavalleypreserve.org/rosemary-spiritual-meaning/

The druid next door — the magick of Rosemary. (2019, July 7). Tumblr.com. https://thedruidnextdoor.tumblr.com/post/186116542942/the-magick-of-rosemary/amp

What is Frankincense Oil? The Benefits and Uses of Frankincense Oil. (n.d.-a). Saje US. https://www.saje.com/ingredient-garden-frankincense.html

What is Frankincense Oil? The Benefits and Uses of Frankincense Oil. (n.d.-b). Saje US. https://www.saje.com/ingredient-garden-frankincense.html

What is Smudging and How do I Smudge? (2016, June 7). Sage Goddess. https://www.sagegoddess.com/how-do-i-smudge/

White, A. (2022, August 28). 10 benefits of burning sage, how to get started, and more. Healthline. https://www.healthline.com/health/benefits-of-burning-sage

Wigington, P. (2013, May 13). The magic and myths of mugwort. Learn Religions. https://www.learnreligions.com/using-mugwort-in-magic-2562031

Wigington, P. (2014, April 13). Frankincense. Learn Religions. https://www.learnreligions.com/magic-and-folklore-of-frankincense-2562024

Wigington, P. (2015a, October 31). Chamomile. Learn Religions. https://www.learnreligions.com/chamomile-2562019

Wigington, P. (2015b, November 29). Rosemary. Learn Religions. https://www.learnreligions.com/rosemary-2562035

Ibiene. (2020, March 15). African signs and symbols: come learn what they mean.... Ibiene.Com. https://ibiene.com/africa/african-signs-and-symbols-come-learn-what-they-mean/

tommy. (2019, April 18). 16 Celtic/scottish Symbols and meanings. Harreira | Everything Pirates. https://harreira.com/symbol/16-celtic-symbols-in-ancient-times/

Secrets & Symbols: Kabbalah Jewelry Explained. (2018, April 1). Baltinester Jewelry & Judaica. https://www.baltinesterjewelry.com/kabbalistic-themes/

O'Hara, K. (2022, January 10). 15 Celtic Symbols and Meanings (An Irishman's 2022 Guide). The Irish Road Trip. https://www.theirishroadtrip.com/celtic-symbols-and-meanings/

8 FAMOUS NORSE SYMBOLS AND THEIR MEANINGS. (n.d.). Reykjaviktouristinfo.Is. https://blog.reykjaviktouristinfo.is/2021/12/8-famous-norse-symbols-and-their-meanings/

African Symbols: Adinkra. (n.d.). Uwm.Edu. https://uwm.edu/african-diaspora-studies/wp-content/uploads/sites/203/2015/06/Symbols-Adinkra-and-VeVe.pdf

Wecker, M. (2008, October 28). What Is A Hamsa? My Jewish Learning. https://www.myjewishlearning.com/article/hamsa/

Rhys, D. (2020, September 10). Serpent Symbolism and Meaning. Symbol Sage. https://symbolsage.com/serpents-meaning-and-symbolism/

How To Cleanse & Charge Amulets, Talisman, and Charms. (n.d.). Magicksymbols. https://magicksymbols.com/blogs/news/how-to-cleanse-charge-amulets-talisman-and-charms

Coen, C. D. (2022, July 20). Get your mojo working. Weird, Wacky, & Wild. https://www.weirdsouth.com/post/get-your-mojo-working

Huanaco, F. (2019, December 12). Free book of spells PDF: Printable rituals, potions & spells. Spells8. https://spells8.com/free-book-of-spells-pdf/

Lacy, D. (n.d.). Crafty Thursday: DIY Gris Gris bags. Mysteryplayground.net. http://www.mysteryplayground.net/2016/02/crafty-thursday-diy-gris-gris-bags.html

Pham, O. (2022, September 9). Runes, Norse magic, and magical content. Wondrium Daily. https://www.wondriumdaily.com/runes-norse-magic-and-magical-content/

Hardy, J. (2022, July 2). 12 African gods and goddesses: The Orisha pantheon. History Cooperative; The History Cooperative. https://historycooperative.org/african-gods-and-goddesses/

López, J. S. (2021, October 27). Obatala – supreme Yoruba deity. Symbol Sage. https://symbolsage.com/obatala-yoruba-deity/

Ogun. (n.d.). Mythencyclopedia.com. http://www.mythencyclopedia.com/Ni-Pa/Ogun.html

Tabalia, J. (2021, April 22). 12 famous African goddesses and gods with mind-blowing history. Briefly; Briefly.co.za. https://briefly.co.za/48019-12-famous-african-goddesses-gods-mind-blowing-history.html